A Massive Dose *of*
MOTIVATION

INFORMATION, IDEAS AND INSIGHT

THAT WILL GET YOU UP, OUT AND MOVING

TOWARD YOUR PERSONAL AND PROFESSIONAL GOALS

Copyright© 2006

Table of Contents

Table of Contents (continued)

WHILE OTHERS MAY

SIDETRACK YOUR AMBITIONS

NOT A FEW TIMES,

REMEMBER THAT DISCOURAGEMENT

MOST FREQUENTLY

COMES FROM

WITHIN.

Alfredo Robledo

www.GrapevineCPA.com

The American Experience and The American Dream are alive in Alfredo Robledo. Starting from humble beginnings, his father arriving in the US as a migrant farm worker, Alfredo saw, first hand, the benefits of starting a business. While the family diner which his mother started no longer exists, its' legacy continues in the homes and the educations that were funded from the wages paid out. His Mother's legacy is continues to be a role model to others forming their own businesses.

Today Alfredo Robledo lives and works in Grapevine, Texas — right outside of DFW airport. He is both a Certified Managerial Accountant and a Certified Public Accountant. His accounting firm serves individuals and business in various stages of development and prosperity. Alfredo is passionate about helping businesses grow and prosper and for our citizens to reach thier financial goals.

Alfredo speaks in on a number of business topics. His favorite subject is how to end the self imposed enslavement to lenders. He believes in the power of bettering our nation by touching one family at a time.

Alfredo can be reached at Alfredo@GrapevineCPA.com.

To Serve and Nurture

"Ask Not What Your Country Can Do For You..."
— J. F. Kennedy

What is the largest check that you have ever written? I wrote my largest a few years ago while I was wrapping up my mother's estate. I spent years learning how to minimize my clients' taxes, and offered to use that knowledge for my mother's benefit. My mother, however, simply asked that my aunt be allowed to live in her house and refused all of the fancy trusts, devices, and other clever dodges. As a result, I needed to pay the inheritance taxes and wrote checks to the State of California and the US Treasury totaling *one hundred thirty thousand dollars* —not a small sum.

As I wrote those checks, a feeling of absolute gratitude came over me. I was incredibly thankful that our family received so many opportunities from this nation and from our community. I then thought of how my life might have been had I been born a few hundred miles to the south. I was reminded of my younger self's dreams and beliefs about this country, and thus began a subconscious shift that would, over the next several years, move me closer to my dreams.

My life has never been easy, and my childhood expectations were simple. I spent my formative years, from second grade onwards, working in my family's tortilla factory and restaurant. Our family lived the immigrants' version of the American Dream: start with nothing and achieve a good life through working long, hard hours. Learning to be disciplined greatly benefited my brother, sister, and me: we were the first in our extended family to graduate from college and begin our own success stories. My brother pursuing a Ph.D. from the University of California at Berkeley; my sister immigrated to Peru to become a violinist with the Peruvian National Symphony; I became a professional, earning the credentials of both a Certified Public Accountant and a Certified Managerial Accountant.

Early in my career, I thought I was following my dreams, when in fact I wasn't listening to them at all. Instead, I allowed myself to be seduced by other people's dreams, worked my tail off trying to achieve them, and ultimately found myself negating many of my hopes and aspirations because they didn't "fit" others' ideals.

One notable example occurred during college, when I worked as a Revenue Agent intern with the Internal Revenue Service, learning tax rules and regulations. My professors and peers constantly reminded me that this internship was somehow unsatisfactory, and that I needed to do something else more prestigious. After graduation, I took their advice and took a position with one of the Big Eight accounting firms. I was seduced by the nearly doubling of my salary, the prestigious address, the exclusive lunch and dinner clubs, and the accolades from my formerly critical professors and peers.

Despite the outward prestige, I found that this job had greatly diminished my professional responsibility, independence, decision-making, and self-confidence. Furthermore, the hours were crazy and the pressure to complete audit work under budget was immense. Many good people came to work at that firm right out of college, but most of these bright men and women left as soon as their two-year apprenticeship was completed. After one season on the audit staff and another in the tax department, my spirit was dying. I hated going to work each day. I realized that it was time to do something different.

While I saw that this was another opportunity to follow my dreams, I did not know what those dreams were. I had inklings but did not explore the options; I lacked the confidence and conviction to set out in a singular career direction. I wanted to keep my options open in order to avoid being "stuck" doing one job for the rest of my life. Thinking back, I now see that I really did know what I wanted all along, but was too immature to pursue it then.

In 1980, I moved to Texas during the "go-go" times in the oil business, of which I soon became a part. My Spanish language abilities, a summer session at the Universidad de las Americas, and the Big Eight experience helped me get a position with a major oil exploration company's international internal audit staff — an exhilarating experience for a young man. For the next several years, I enjoyed foreign travel to Peru, Bolivia, and Mexico, with side trips to Argentina and Chile. Domestic assignments took me to Los Angles, Bakersfield, and the coal mines of Kentucky and West Virginia.

The adventure of these assignments, which due to my age and level of experience would not have been offered to me in the United States, seduced me all over again. Because I was willing to go "in country" for long assignments, and at times enter into harm's way, I was given the opportunity to learn, observe, and be a part of business activities that would otherwise have taken me another ten to fifteen years to experience.

This valuable experience, however, came with a price: loneliness. Being "in country" for months at a time soon led me to give up my home in Texas. All of my worldly belongings were either crammed into my car, which was left in the office parking lot, or in my suitcases. Giving up my home made keeping in touch with my loved ones extremely difficult. 25 years ago the now-unquestioned convenience of e-mail did not exist, and the then-available communication methods of "snail mail", cables and couriers were inconvenient, expensive, and slow.

Loneliness became a constant, aching pull at my heart. I soon rationalized it as a theoretical cost of doing business. But loneliness is very real, as were its effects on my soul. It caused a further negation of my dreams and, instead, an embracing of the company's goals and objects. In retrospect, I am amazed at how much hardship I endured for the sake of playing my part in a big organization.

The end was abrupt. One day in October, more than half of the 60-person staff was recalled to Houston for an important meeting. The meeting lasted only long enough for the department manager to state, "Your services are no longer needed". A representative from personnel then handed out severance packages, and later, fifteen armed security guards watched over us as we cleared out our desks then escorted us to our cars. As I carried my boxes to my car, I thought, "What a nice way to repay loyalty… tossed out into an 11.5% unemployment market."

Losing the job was actually another opportunity to change direction and follow my dreams, but I did not take advantage of it. Instead, I simply replaced one international employer for another, and spent another seven years in international finance. The pace of travel was severe at times. Overseas trips would last for six weeks at a time, returning back to Dallas for five nights before going overseas for another six weeks to handle some "emergency". During this time, by some miracle, I met a lady who became my wife and together we brought our first of two endearing, precious children into the world. Her birth ended my ten-year career in international business; I discovered that all of the excitement and intrigue of foreign travel (as well as the years I invested in South American business) seemed empty and meaningless when compared to the riches of being a husband and father. I simply did not want to be away from my family for weeks at a time.

I spent the next nine years working for a large beverage company. These were years of constant "right sizing" — a code name for downsizing. During that time I had seven different bosses, and underwent five reorganizations. There was frequent turnover in the leadership of most departments and locations. A new corporate manager would arrive one day and leave shortly there after. With each new temporary occupant of the corner office came the promises to develop and improve the department, which really meant, "let's see how much *more* work you can get done with fewer people and little to no new technology, training, or financial incentives". After a while, I began to hope that the new managers would simply not mess things up too badly, because I would still be there after they left. After nine years, I had enough and relieved to lose my job during the next reorganization.

The next stop was at a national company owned by a huge foreign corporation with several companies operating in almost every country in the world. My short-term assignment was to put the financial manger's desk in order. However, things took another direction and I wound up on the path to rediscovering my soul.

At that company, I worked for three separate general managers. The first two general managers purposefully forced me to rediscover who I was and what values I cherished; the last manager, on the other hand, taught me why troops in combat will, at times, turn on their inexperienced officers.

Art, the first location manager, possessed a deep understanding of organizational behavior, human dynamics, leadership skills, and leadership training. While he never attended college, his knowledge of these topics was deeper and broader than most doctoral candidates. After spending years alongside his Ph.D. boss training company leaders, he was assigned to put theory into practice by leading a less than stellar distribution center. He turned it into one of the best locations in the United States.

What an experience it was to work for someone who constantly forced me to think about my leadership styles and decision-making values! He constantly pointed out the unintended consequences of actions and decisions, as well as inaction and indecisiveness. His constant examination of potential legacy was a new concept to me. His insistence that I examine my core values and the legacy I was forming through my daily actions was both intriguing and challenging.

After a year or so, Art was moved back into leadership training. His replacement, Hugo, is a true gentleman and an aggressive business leader. He is demanding and at times delivered a wicked butt-chewing. But, he deeply values and rewards the dedication of his front line and mangers. His willingness to accept challenges and rally the troops around the challenge is remarkable. What truly made him special and worthy of my personal loyalty was his continuous passing of the credit to his team. Hugo is frequently on the front lines, at times taking hits, fighting for resources, knocking down barriers, and being the head cheerleader for the distribution center employees.

Hugo's leadership was noticed and he was transferred to a larger market to lead a larger organization. Shortly thereafter a corporate reorganization combined business groups, which deeply affected our distribution center.

A new manager was assigned as part of a reorganization slotting. The fit was awkward and unsettling, and I saw a train-wreck approaching at full steam. By the end of the year he fired me — about three weeks before I had planned to quit. Within just months, 80% of the original managers left the company as well.

I learned several things while working with Art, Hugo and the last guy. I learned that I still believe in and value the cadet honor code from the teenage years I spent in the Civil Air Patrol. I learned what focusing on my leadership skills could accomplish. I learned the value and joy of serving others. And I learned just how all too human my corporate leaders really were.

From all of my corporate experiences, I learned to hate blind obedience to the "mantra of the day" corporations' demand of their employees. I still puzzle over why American workers can be the most productive in the world, yet not be allowed to tell their employers that maybe; just maybe, the Emperor has no clothes on.

Thanks in part to Hugo's influence; I found that my mother's passing pushed me to focus on my legacy, which caused me to come to terms with my dreams. I finally accepted that I no longer wanted to be a part of corporate America. The role choked my talents, limited my contributions, and corralled my creativity. Equally, the constant valuing of a person's political correctness over their significant contributions grated on my values. There are many good managers in Corporate America who are loyal to there employees and customers. Some are exceptional. For me it was time to serve a different master. It was time to form a career that allowed me to make choices I could be proud of; choices in which I risk my own capital for the goals I value and make decisions that are creating a positive legacy.

I now work to serve America — the greatest country in the world. The great human experiment that started in 1776 continues to develop and ferment, and reshape and redefine itself. The real leadership of this country has never been the many elected office holders. Our leadership has always been the men and women who go to work each and every day and contribute to our communities. This group is made up of several million individuals who give of themselves so that kids can learn, congregations can receive spiritual guidance, police and fire forces get adequate equipment and training, and the small business owners. These people that risk their life savings to build small businesses, which in turn provides employment, allowing families achieve their slice of the American Dream of their own.

This country gave me so many wonderful opportunities. It gave me an identity. It offered a chance for a great education, tremendous personal freedoms, and the right to decide what is best for me and my family. It is now my obligation to serve America, not in uniform as my nephew did on foreign sands, but by simply doing what I can to improve the American Dream for my clients, their employees, the families of the employees, and our communities.

Today I serve by sharing my knowledge and my time with those who are setting up and growing their business. I know first-hand that America, the American Dream, and the American spirit touches one person at a time; I have been that person. I have seen first-hand that decent paychecks lead to saving for a home, providing for a child's education, buying a desired luxury item, or funding one's retirement plan. By helping one client better their business and hire one more permanent, full-time employee at a decent wage, I can help one more family claim their American Dream.

My profession feeds my soul and delivers great joy as I learn the life stories of people with whom I work, discover their drive to build businesses, and learn see the world through their eyes. The empowerment I feel is incredible. Instead of suffocating in a corporate setting, I am liberated to be myself and apply my God-given skills to help others grow dreams and leave legacies of their own

45 years ago, a young American President, standing hatless on a cold January day in Washington, D.C., implored his fellow citizens to "ask not what your county can do for you; ask what you can do for your country."

Well, Mister President, it took me a while, but I am reporting for duty. 🔺

Connie Houston

c_houston@shaw.ca

www.conniehouston.com

Connie's personal story serves as the foundation for her "DARE To Change Your Life" message.

Her message encourages and empowers individuals to create a rich and meaningful life.

Former Social Worker and Professional Parent Trainer for a Treatment Foster Care program for over a decade, Connie now delivers her message to community groups, school programs and audiences around the province.

Her background as a parenting and child development expert help her genuinely touch parents and children with the message that they are the greatest miracle in the world and capable of achieving their goals and aspirations.

A successful Internet entrepreneur, she also helps other women start home businesses to achieve financial and emotional freedom.

She currently resides in beautiful Alberta, Canada with her husband and three children—David, Matthew and Michael.

For a list of recommended reading material and website links, please visit Connie at her website:

www.conniehouston.com
c_houston@shaw.ca

D.A.R.E. To Change Your Life!

Desperate housewives. I never thought that I would end up living that cliché. I never thought that I would be one of the millions of people who wake up one morning asking, "Is this all there is to life??" I had always believed that everything happens for a reason, and I tried to cling to that belief while my world seemed to be falling apart around me. And though I continued to give thanks daily for the truly important things in my life, (health and children) I was finding it harder and harder to see the stars as I sank into the darkness of depression.

Two years earlier, I had been working as a successful social worker, juggling a part-time job, three boys (two toddlers and a teenager) and a marriage to a man who worked out of town most of the time, all of which left me exhausted but content. I loved encouraging others, and being a mother was everything I had always dreamed of. Life was comfortable, rather boring, but securely routine.

Two months after receiving a glowing recommendation and a promotion at work, I was suddenly terminated from my position without justification or reason. I spiraled into depression. My husband turned to alcohol and gambling. The security that I had built as a single mother of twenty-one, including going back to college and graduating and building my career, had vanished. I considered leaving my husband but realized that in my current financial situation, the children and I would be homeless within two months. My pride and my shame kept me from asking for help from family members. I began to feel desperate—trapped in a life that I had not pictured myself living. I knew only one thing for certain—something had to change. And I was the one who had to do it.

Because I had completely isolated myself, as one tends to do when living with an alcoholic and/or depression, I turned to the Internet to reach out for anonymous support. That is when my life started to change.

When I realized that I needed to make a change, I decided the best way to become happy and successful was to find happy and successful people and study their lives. I completely immersed myself in self-improvement tools. I read daily, listened to audios, wrote goals for myself, took courses on the Internet, and attended motivational conference calls on the computer. I stopped watching television— other than the Amazing Race! Studies have shown that ninety percent of television programming has a negative influence on your life, so get out of the rut!

When I began my quest, I kept searching for the magical, quick-fix cure in book after book, looking for the secrets to success and happiness. I felt like I was building a puzzle, and while I had all the pieces (and some of them were even in place), I couldn't get the whole picture because I didn't have the box with the picture on it. But I continued to surround myself with positive influences, living vicariously through others' successes in books and on the Internet, and I learned the truth in the saying, "When the student is ready, the teacher will appear," because that is when Johnny Wimbrey and Kevin Bracy entered my life via long distance phone calls. What a blessing! With their support, and guidance, I finally started to get the "big picture."

The more I read, and listened to, the more it reinforced the pattern that was emerging for me. Every single great teacher, writer, and leader in history, from Jesus to Ghandi to Henry Ford, held the same philosophy on achieving a happy, successful life: "Our thoughts determine our actions." The Bible is full of references to support this, such as "As a man thinketh in his heart, so is he." (Proverbs 23:7) Ford summed up in his famous quote, "Whether you think you can, or think you can't, you are right."

So basically I concluded that our lives are completely defined by this concept—*we become what we think about!* I finally GOT IT, and my life began to change. Armed with new hope, and a changed attitude, I was able to overcome those circumstances that I had previously considered obstacles. I was on my way to a richer, more meaningful life.

What about you? Where are you at in your search for a happier life? Is life just dragging you along?

Or, are you ready to take control and make some changes?

Here are a few pointers to help you get started. You may think that many of the following concepts are not new or earth-shattering. But read them with an open, searching heart, and if your hunger is deep enough, they can help you change your life, too.

The D.A.R.E. Principles:
(The Double Dare!)

D—DECISION: You need to decide that something is not right in your life and you want to change it. If you don't know there is a problem, or don't care if there is, nothing will change. How important is it to you to improve your life? Human beings are creatures of comfort and there is nothing more comfortable than a familiar routine. Even when our routine (life) isn't all that comfortable, we resist change. Sometimes it is only when we find ourselves in circumstances that are so unbearably painful, that we consider change. Sometimes when things happen that are beyond your control, you have no choice. It's either continue living with agonizing pain (which may be physical, emotional or spiritual), or make a change. One of my favorite quotes is from Einstein, "The definition of insanity is doing the same thing over and over again, and expecting a different result."

D—DREAM: Discover your dream. You need to find your dreams again. What excited you when you were young? What would you be doing if you never had to worry about money again? Spend some time thinking about this. Many of our dreams are covered in dust. Invest time in yourself by learning what your dreams are. **You are worth it.** Dream so big that it's going to take a miracle to get it! Do you know that most people spend more money on gas for their vehicle every month than they do on their own self-development? What about you? Do you take better care of your bathroom, even your toilet, than you do of yourself and your dreams? Invest in something that really matters— yourself!

A—ATTITUDE: Check yours. If you know that, "You are what you think," how positive is your outlook on life? What dominates your thoughts? You can't expect positive results when you spend 10 minutes a day thinking positively… and the remaining 14 waking hours dwelling on negative outcomes! The bottom line is that a little bit of positive thinking doesn't produce positive results. You can't do a few minutes of exercise once a week and expect to be physically fit. Look at positive thinking the same way. A little bit just doesn't get the job done. Instead, you must take control of your mental activity and think positively throughout each and every day until it becomes a habit. Fact—Your beliefs brought you to where you are today, and your thinking from this point forward will take you to where you'll be in the future.

A—ACTION: You MUST take action! You will never reach your dreams or goals if you are merely thinking about them. If you are serious about making changes/improvements in your life, you will need to make a plan and then start taking baby steps to get there. Kevin often said, "You don't have to get it right, you just have to get it going." He also quoted Les Brown, "Just jump and your wings will grow on the way down!" When I began my quest, I didn't have a clue what I was doing but I had faith, so I made the leap. Sometimes it's hard to have faith or courage, and you just need to trust that the way will become clear. Kevin also taught me that God honors commitment. When you make a commitment and are willing to do whatever it takes, regardless of your obstacles, you begin to attract the people and circumstances necessary to accomplish your goal. You don't have to know at the outset how to achieve your goal. Just be open to new opportunities and it will come to you. Be patient with yourself—even slow motion is better than no motion.

R—REVIEW: Do a quick mental check-up daily. Ask yourself, "Did I do something today that moved me closer to my goal?" If you are frustrated or confused, go back to WHY you want to change. How STRONG is your why? Write your goals down, along with your deadline for reaching them. Research has proven that people who write their goals down are much more likely to achieve them. Pat yourself on the back for the small (or large) steps you have already taken.

R—REPETITION: When you first begin making changes in your life, it won't be comfortable. Growth can be painful. Think about the last time you used muscles that you haven't used for a long time. When you continue to use them, however, the pain goes away. When you're gripped by fear and anxiety, it's usually because you're stepping out of your comfort zone. Confront your fears and be willing to stretch yourself and expand your comfort zone. Consider the price you pay when you back away from your fears that are standing in the way of your growth. Here's what happens: your self-esteem is lowered, you feel powerless and frustrated, you sabotage your success and you lead a boring, uneventful life. It's your choice. There's a price to pay if you want to make things better, and a price you'll pay for just leaving things as they are. The good news is that your courage muscle can be developed just like any other muscle—with exercise. When you do an activity outside of your comfort zone a few times, it becomes part of your comfort zone. You will not develop your abilities to the fullest unless you're willing to be uncomfortable. Life doesn't reward those who refuse to expose themselves to difficulties and challenges. Confront your fears, make a decision to overcome your adversity. We all have obstacles in our life, don't let yours control you.

E—EXPECTATION: There is a purpose for your life! There is only one YOU in the entire world and no one can do what you are meant to do better than you. You deserve to be happy and successful. You have greatness within you… and your attitude is the key to unlocking that potential. Changing your attitude and your expectations will change your life. Has anyone told you lately that you are the greatest miracle in the world? You truly are. Napoleon Hill said, "What the mind can conceive and believe, the mind can achieve." Johnny and Kevin taught me a very valuable lesson—**Never let someone else define your world because it will always be smaller than the world you would have created.** Remember to dream so big that it's going to take a miracle to get. Expect miracles and you will get them!

E—ENTHUSIASM: Get excited about your life! You are on the path to success and the journey is an exciting one. You have the power to do and be whatever you want to do and be. You have greatness within you! Get around positive people who will celebrate you and all your accomplishments throughout your journey. Don't hang around negative people who tolerate you and drain the life and energy from you. Beware of "life-suckers", there are many out there! Find successful people who share your vision and beliefs, even if you have to reach out anonymously, as I did. If a stay-at-home mother without a vehicle could do it, so can you!

It is my deepest desire to reach out and spread hope to others who are still struggling. I struggled alone for a long time and I don't want you to suffer alone. You are not alone. Whatever obstacles you need to overcome in your life, someone else is going through the same thing. But you need to reach out. When you do, amazing things will start to happen.

I applaud you for taking the time to read this book. It shows that you're truly interested in developing your incredible potential. Yet, reading this book is only the first step to living the life you want to live. When you focus on these ideas—and take action to implement them—you're on the way to creating some exciting breakthroughs in your life. Keep in mind that success and failure in life are guaranteed—the choice is up to you. I challenge you now—I dare you to change your life! ♠

Dan O'Dell

563-210-4356

thinkingrich@aol.com

Dan O'Dell is a man of diverse backgrounds and many different talents. Being raised in a military household meant being exposed to all four corners of the United States during his childhood formative years. He learned early to face adversity by supporting himself with paper routes and odd jobs. At the age of twelve he was hanging sheetrock for five dollars a day in Texas. The building trades followed leading to successful contracting businesses.

As a young man he knew he had a special gift to inspire others through the power of the spoken word. By the age of twenty five he had served three small Churches and spent two years on the radio following Paul Harvey on a daily fifteen minute broadcast called MOMENTS OF TRUTH. Years later he produced thirty six half hour radio broadcasts delivered on a major station in the Dallas-Fort Worth Metroplex during prime time on Sunday Morning.

Business presentations in the Network Marketing Industry led to team training sessions, Regional events, and then National Conventions as a keynote speaker.

Dan's life mission is to master, communicate, and inspire excellence in human development. He is a graduate of the "University of Hard Knocks" and speaks with loving authority as one who has learned it is not easy to find happiness within your self, the source of it, and impossible to find it anywhere else. Favorite subjects include THE POWER OF THOUGHT, INNER LIGHT-OUTER WEALTH, THE POWER OF INTENTION, and THE POWER OF NOW. He is a student of old English "New Thought" principles and the science of personal achievement. Napoleon Hill, James Allen, and Earl Nightingale are his heroes.

Dan O'Dell is managing director of THINKING RICH ENTERPRISES and is committed to presenting old secrets for new inspiration.

Contact information:
thinkingrich@aol.com
563-210-4356

Your Belief Makes It Happen!

An Open Letter to the Seeker of Self Empowerment
by Dan O'Dell

October, 2005

Dear Seeker,

Believing you have acquired *A MASSIVE DOSE OF MOTIVATION* as a result of a deep desire within your being to be, do and have more in your life, leads me to share with you a few simple thoughts which have been of life-shaping value to me. Over the years I have operated on the principles that follow to accomplish outstanding achievements the likes of which most men, generally speaking, never enjoy.

For instance, in 1975 I walked on to a one hundred fifty acre site between Wichita Falls and Burkburnett, Texas where the new AC SPARK PLUG plant was being constructed. Drilled Piers were just being started for the first of the manufacturing buildings. I was the first carpenter to be hired and only twenty seven years old. It was not long before the project accelerated and several more phases started. Soon a position opened up for an on site Project Manager with Construction Cost Accounting and Construction Estimating experience. I had several years of that type of experience with two smaller contractors in the area previously. I had no idea at the time I piped up, "I can do that. Let me do it," what I was about to take on. They promoted me, set up my office in a mobile home (right in the middle of the site) and I managed the project for the next two years.

I simply had no doubts that I could do it. No one told me I really ought to have years of engineering training and a series of large projects under my belt before taking on such responsibility. No one told me I was not equipped to do what I did. I simply believed if I could see it, I could build it. Even though I had no idea what I was about to be looking at! I did not know, at the beginning, the project would include one million square feet under roof, a railroad spur, a train dump pit, a chilled water utility trestle system, a waste water treatment plant and a large office building! I ended up managing fourteen million dollars worth of construction under seven different simultaneous contracts, at the same time, with an average of one hundred contract change orders each. There were one hundred fifty men on site at the zenith. My belief made it happen.

If you look back over your life time you will recall events that are similar in nature as it relates to a certain achievement. You simply believed you could accomplish your goal, acted like it and notwithstanding a multitude of unforeseen obstacles carried on to the completion. Success leaves clues and they are found in such cases by those who look for them with eyes to see.

I am mindful of the words of Frank Lloyd Wright: *"The thing always happens that you really believe in: and the belief in a thing makes it happen!"*

Herein abides the root principle of your personal successes. The quality, extent, and intensity of your *"belief in a thing makes it happen."*

One of the greatest examples of this came to me, unasked for, on the news, in the winter of 2002. A home movie was being shown which had been taken in 1991. It pictured a five year old little girl with pigtails, who voiced her own self-fulfilling prophecy. It sounded like this: *"I want to go to the Olympics and win a gold medal. I can't wait to do THAT."*

There was no question in her mind. No doubt to consider. She simply could not *"wait to do THAT."* In her mind, it was as good as done. The only issue was how long it would take to get there. I got up from my place and wrote this down. To this day I often carry it with me on a 3x5 note card and have long since memorized it. I knew I had just heard the secret of success from the mouth of a five year old!

A few days later, I watched the Olympic Figure Skating Championships. Just before she took the ice, this same little girl, had witnessed two of the worlds' greatest figure skaters perform to near perfection and she had to follow them.

After eleven years of training and momentarily doubting her ability to win, she decided (as she put it): *"to go out there and have the time of my life."*

In the 2002 Winter Olympics, at the age of 16, Sarah Hughes won the gold medal! You see, *"The thing always happens that you really believe in: and the belief in the thing makes it happen!"*

In order to further open this principle to your view, I have included a brief series of quotations by some of my favorite authors for your encouragement. The first of which is JESUS CHRIST, who taught the following simple truths:

"According to thy faith be it unto thee."
MATHEW 9:19

"ALL THINGS are possible to him that BELIEVETH!"
MARK 9:23

Not long afterwards the Apostle Paul wrote to the Hebrews (11:1) and explained, *"Faith is the substance of things hoped for, the evidence of things not seen."* I feel safe here in adding the word "yet" without doing damage to the intent of the text.

Moving forward in time to 1937, after having interviewed several hundred of America's most successful business men (including Henry Ford and W. Clement Stone) Napoleon Hill said it like this:

"ANY dominant idea, plan, or purpose that you hold in your mind through repetition of thought, mixed with a burning desire for its realization, is taken over by the sub-conscious mind and acted upon through whatever logical and natural means is available."

In his book, *THINK AND GROW RICH*, he quoted Thomas Edison as saying: *"Whatever the mind can conceive and believe, it can achieve."* Can you imagine what our world would be like if he had not believed this? What if he had stopped his experiments at 9,950 as compared to going on to 10,000?

"You can think yourself into disaster or think yourself into victory and happiness." "Your sub-conscious mind can feed upon random thoughts of defeat or upon thoughts of success and riches. The choice is yours!"

I invite you to consider with me for a moment, *"Any dominant idea, plan or purpose"*, *"Whatever the mind can conceive and believe it can achieve."* Is it possible, my dear reader, both poverty and riches are the offspring of our thoughts? Is it possible our thoughts only reflect what we really BELIEVE? Can we choose what we really believe? And if so, what choices must we therefore make if we, indeed, become what we think about?

Earl Nightingale was highly effected at the youthful age of 19 when he discovered a copy of James Allen's little book titled *AS A MAN THINKETH*. Years later he wrote and recorded the first speech to become a Gold Record by selling over a million copies! He called it *THE STRANGEST SECRET*. In his speech his principle thought was, *"Human thoughts have a tendency to transform themselves into their physical equivalent."* I will never forget hearing the golden voice of Earl Nightingale making this statement on an audio tape as I was driving toward Fort Smith, Arkansas in the spring of 2000. *"Human thoughts have a tendency to transform themselves into their physical equivalent."* I listened to it several more times and stopped the tape player. I asked myself, how could this be so? How can that which is intangible become a physical reality? And, if it is so, whether I understand it or not, I must learn to think differently in order to get different results in my life.

Mary Kay Ash built a network marketing empire, selling cosmetics. One of her favorite motivational statements was: *"What you think about you bring about."*

A few years ago Patrick Porter wrote an enlightening book titled *AWAKEN THE GENIUS (Mind technology for the 21st century)*. The central premise of which was, *"What you believe will come to pass as a reality"* and *"The law of the mind is the law of BELIEF."*

In his most recent book entitled *THE POWER OF INTENTION* (sub titled: How to co-create your world your way) Wayne Dyer makes a remarkable statement saying: *"Contemplate yourself as being surrounded by the conditions you intend to produce."* Sense it. Feel it, as if it is a reality.

I have read and re-read this book, this year, many times. It has been an incredible journey within for me. My beliefs have been challenged, transcended, and centered upon my Divine Source. The very fact I am now seated in front of the word processor writing this letter, is a result of this journey. My *"dominant ideas, plans or purposes"* are being realized because the quality, extent, and intensity of my BELIEFS have grown.

Mr. Dyer identifies *"highly realized people"* as those who are "connected" to their Source. This "connection" is more than positional. It is experiential. It is a way of life for them. It is a moment by moment awareness of their spiritual union with their Source. *"They* (Connectors) *can see what it is they intend to manifest into their lives, as if it had already materialized, and for them, because its so real in their thoughts, its their reality."*

"These highly realized people think from the end, experiencing what they wish to intend before it shows up in material form!"

They what? They think from the end and act that way. Since the thing always happens that you really believe in you might as well act on your positive *"dominant ideas, plans or purposes"* as if they have already materialized!

I am reminded of what the young ministerial student asked the Senior Pastor one day when he concluded his sermon on FAITH, *"What do you do when you don't have faith?"*

The Senior Pastor replied with a big smile on his face: *"Act that way!"*

How could this be? Acting upon those positive and passionate emotions as if they already exist sends a signal to the subconscious mind and all of your creative juices start to flow towards the fulfillment of your desires *"through whatever logical and natural means is available."* It does not matter were you are or what your circumstance may be. Your belief makes it happen!

In light of the fact everything around us (that now is) began as a creative thought and thoughts held in your mind in a repetitive way *"transform themselves into their physical equivalent"* I suggest the following for your consideration:

WHAT IF you started the day every day with this self-fulfilling prophecy, sensing, feeling and believing it to be your present reality? What if several times a day you found a few moments to build-up yourself by reciting the following affirmation:

"I AM INSEPARABLY CONNECTED TO AND IN ARMONY WITH MY DIVINE SOURCE."

"My source is: Creative, Kind, Loving, Beautiful, always Expanding, Abundant without limits, and Receptive to all life."

"I am whole and perfect as I was created."

"I attract success and abundance into my life, because that is who I am!"

"As my Source is so am I."

"I am Creative, Kind, Loving, Beautiful, always Expanding, Abundant without limits, and Receptive to all life."

"My Source and I are one."

"I love my Source."

"I LOVE ME!"

If you will do this for twenty one days you will experience a dramatic change in the way you feel about your self. You are worth the effort it will take to write this down on note cards and read it to yourself morning, noon and just before going to sleep at night. In a few days you will have it memorized. As you meditate on the meaning of these words (to you individually) the ramifications of them will begin to appear. If you commit to this exercise you will begin to experience an awakening of dormant powers, faculties and talents within your SELF and a new sense of BEING will occur. The end result will be astonishing to you. You are worth it. The time you spend on your self will come back to you many times over with a new sense of who you are and what you are about.

Remember, we become what we think about. What we think about repetitively is what we really believe. What we really believe will come to pass in our life as a reality. This being so, it is very important for us to do for ourselves what we must do to challenge, transcend, and intensify the quality of our belief in who and what we are in order to go beyond and out of the ordinary.

My dear reader, you already know these things. Resident within you is all of the knowledge, creativity, love, kindness, courage, wisdom, and talents you need to take you to the next level in you life. You have the power within you to build up your own belief factor in who you are and what you are about. I submit, you are a greater person, by far, than you have ever dreamed your self to be. Your belief will make it happen!

James Allen included this poem in his little book *AS A MAN THINKETH* over one hundred years ago. I trust it will do for you what it has done for me.

> *"Mind is the master power that moulds and makes,*
> *And man is mind and evermore he takes,*
> *The tool of thought, and shaping what he wills,*
> *Brings forth a thousand joys, a thousand ills,*
> *He thinks in secret and it comes to pass,*
> *Environment is but his looking glass."*

In 1991 there was a little five-year-old girl with pigtails who voiced her own self-fulfilling prophecy. It sounded like this: *"I want to go to the Olympics and win a gold medal. I can't wait to do THAT"*

Eleven years later, that same little girl, now sixteen years old, won the Olympic Gold Medal at the ladies figure skating Championships because *"The thing always happens that you really believe in: and the belief in the thing makes it happen!"*

What will your self fulfilling prophecies sound like this year? Where will they take you eleven years from now? You are a creating machine. Look within. See how great you are and do what you must to empower your SELF.

I shall remain, sincerely yours for peace and prosperity.

TO MORE LIFE!

Dan O'Dell, Keynote Speaker
THINKING RICH ENTERPRISES
Presenting Old Secrets for New Inspiration
thinkingrich@aol.com ⬆

Dave Sheffield

Success Recipes International

6 Hillcrest Ct.

Eldridge, IA 52748

563-343-5412

1-800-863-2591

www.theshef.com

Dave Sheffield has touched thousands of people with his electrifying message. He has been called "America's hottest speaking sensation". Dave "The Shef" Sheffield brings boundless energy and connection to his presentations. He is an expert in helping people jump to the next level by using the leadership qualities they already possess. Whether it is leading a family or a billion dollar company; Dave "The Shef" Sheffield's message will drive you to immediate action!

He started his first company at the age of nineteen. He has helped many people and companies reach new heights by utilizing the power of ASK! He is an international author and speaker, his other works include: Unleashing the Leader Within You; Unleashing the Vision Within You; How to Make Great Choices in Not So Great Times; and Body, Mind, Wallet.

A sample of his clients include: Monster.com, Clear Channel Radio, Nikken Health Systems, Saladmaster, Valley Shelter Homes, Gold's Gym, Wisconsin State Guidence Counselors Association, Electrolux…The list goes on.

He can be reached at:

Dave Sheffield
Success Recipes International
6 Hillcrest Ct.
Eldridge, IA 52748
563-343-5412
1-800-863-2591
www.theshef.com

My Momma Just Knew!

When I was 19 years old, working in a factory, I had little to nothing in my name. I was living in my mom's basement and had very little direction in life. One morning before work, my mother gave me Les Brown's "Live Your Dreams" tape. I tried to explain to her that I liked to crank my music up on the way to work and that I just didn't have time to listen to that self-help nonsense. I imagined the tape to be just another one of those "get rich quick" schemes. In her infinite patience, she just told me that if I ever wanted to go anywhere in life, I would have to program positive things into my head. So, to appease her, I took the cassette and placed it in my glove box for what seemed like an eternity.

I was doing the daily grind over and over again. I would drive to work and back, repeating the same schedule every day. What a boring cycle it was. One day I had an exceptionally bad day at work and couldn't wait to get out of there. When my shift was over, I frantically looked for the tape my mother had given me! After five minutes of picking through potato chip wrappers, insurance cards, and heavy metal tapes,

I found the tape. This was a 3rd generation audio, but the content was unbelievable! I learned that Les Brown wasn't born with a silver spoon in his mouth; far from it. Here was a man who was abandoned in a building at birth, held back in school, and labeled "mentally retarded." Yet, here he was sharing the wonderful stories of his life; a situation made possible *because he didn't let the outside world hold him back.* I remember thinking that my own problems were bad, but they were nothing compared to what this man had gone through! He is now one of the top-paid motivational speakers in the world, earning over $30,000 per hour for his time! If he could do it, I figured that I could too! I didn't know how yet, but the motivational seed had been planted. I became a student of success and devoured every positive resource I could find. I listened to every motivational tape I could get my hands on. The public library was a great resource for me, as well.

A strange thing started happening to me. I began to think and act differently, and started looking for ways to improve myself. I was working with people who were trapped in something called the "closed-ended mentality." They would only work as hard as they were paid, and if the company wanted more, they would need to be paid more. The same complaining that I put up with and thought of as normal just a month prior, was now driving me crazy. I tried to share some of my self-help stories stuff to my co-workers, but my advice almost always fell on deaf ears. None of my friends were interested, so I decided that **I was the only one who could work on my own self-improvement.** Jim Rohn says "You can't hire someone to do your push-ups for you".

Shef's lesson: It is possible that you and your current group of peers are not the best source for guidance in your life. You need to expand your circle of leaders and find successful mentors or motivational audios to listen to **every day.**

I began to realize that I was a millionaire in training, but my bank account just hadn't caught up to my ideals yet. My mother was very proud of my new-found interest in self-improvement. We would share parts of our favorite tapes and books and discuss the ones we didn't care for. She told me that a man named Tony Robbins would be coming to Minneapolis in two days, and asked me if I had ever heard of him. I told her that I would love to see him live. It seemed like I could scrap up the cash for either the ticket or the trip, but not both. I decided that if I got there, I'd find a way in. Somehow, I found myself walking around backstage at the arena, hoping for a break. As I looked up, I realized that I was right in front of Tony's green room where he was eating. I stood in the doorway, and remembering all of the training that I had been saturating myself with, I acted as though I was a celebrity there.

"Tony!" I said confidently, "It's great to see you again!" Just then, a security guard with forearms as big as my thighs, and no neck, rushed toward me. Tony stood up and came over, telling the security guard that it was all right. This guy had to be at least seven feet tall! When he shook my hand, his fingers went up past my wrist. I explained to him my financial situation and lack of ticket, even turning my pockets inside out to illustrate my point. "Be my guest," he said. He then thanked me for my persistence and told me to live with passion.

After that evening, I began to have a direction in my life. I decided that the number one cause behind a lack of motivation is a lack of important goals. Dr. Martin Luther King Jr. once said, "If you haven't found something that you'd die for, you really haven't lived." That realization was the beginning of where I am today. I didn't know "how" I would accomplish the many things in life that I was committed to, but I had a whole lot of "why."

A short time after that seminar, I was laid off at IBM. While most people were grumbling about how they would get by, I was thanking my manager for giving me the jumpstart needed to accomplish my dreams. He looked at me funny, and asked me if I had been drinking. I simply explained to him my self improvement journey. Two days after I was laid off, I was hired as a salesman. I had a blast! Not only that, but my new manager, Mike Mckay, was a hard worker, which helped lift my spirits to the next level. I busted my hump selling vacuum cleaners door-to-door. Rain, snow, heat, or sleet…..I was out selling! My motto was, "If it is ever raining or snowing *inside* of the house, I'm outta' there, otherwise, they're buying!" My career blossomed into various levels of management. I have Joe DelVecchio to thank, for teaching me how to understand people's needs and the power of duplication. I have Cleve Gaddis to thank, for helping me reach higher and work harder than I ever thought possible.

If you would be perfectly comfortable staying exactly who you are right now for the remainder of your life, you wouldn't be reading this. Think about the giant within you, the dream you are afraid to act upon, the relationship you are tolerating even if it is abusive, and the limited lifestyle you are settling for. You can't do anything about the past, and you can't directly impact the future, but you have been given the gift of TODAY. I firmly believe that all of us are either growing or dying.

Zig Ziglar says that we are who we are and where we are, because of what we put into our minds. We can change who we are and where we are by changing what we put into our heads.

Shef's lesson: Focus on the why of something instead of the how. The how will show up someday. It is looking for a person with enough passion and dedication to do it justice. Let fear be part of your fuel and it will take you to new heights.

The Personal Trainer

About a year ago, I started working out with a personal trainer. I firmly believe that if you want to accelerate your results in any area of your life, you need to employ the services of someone who is already achieving what you want. You don't need to look at the credentials following someone's name to know whether or not their advice will be helpful. I can look at their body. If they have achieved the results I want, I can learn from them. Matt Wiese is a celebrity trainer, fitness author, and coach. The first thing he did after giving me a brief medical questionnaire, is ask me *what I wanted to achieve out of training.* He said without a specific goal to move toward, we cannot measure our progress and know whether or not we are getting good results. He then gave me a food log. Everything that passed through my lips needed to be written down. *What you put into your body, your body gives you back tenfold.* With that, he sends me on my way.

What a great analogy for life. The information that we put into our bodies will dictate what we get out of our bodies. The information we put into our minds, we will get out of our minds. Watch very carefully that you are not flooding your mind with the poisons of media news, negativity, and heartache. Fill it, instead, with positive books, audios, and people.

Shef's lesson: If you don't think you have any time to improve yourself, just cut out one hour of television per day. In one year, you will add an extra nine working weeks of time to your life!

The Power of the Mentor

I began my journey into the public speaking world with the assistance of a wonderful mentor named Kevin Bracy. He told me that while my own belief in myself hadn't yet kicked in, his belief in me would get me by until it did. Kevin and I have had a wonderful relationship. It wasn't always easy, but always educational. He is doing what I want to do at the level at which I want to do it.

A few months ago, I was being interviewed on the subject of motivation. I thought I did very well in the interview. While the questions seemed to fly by, I thought I shared many brilliant ideas with the audience, even expanding on a number of subjects. The next day, Kevin called me up chewed me up one side and down the other. He told me that while my content was fine, I had spent too much time talking about subjects that I thought were important, rather than answering the questions at hand. "If you do an interview like that in the national media, it will be your last!" His words stung me, but I remembered that even Michael Jordan needed a coach. I'm sure that that relationship wasn't always easy, either. I thanked him for his thoughts and was committed to learn from the experience.

Shef's lesson: When you want to accomplish anything, find someone who is doing what it is that you want to do at the level you want to do it. You will need to pay them for their advice and knowledge, but the power of a coach/mentor will catapult your dreams to new heights. This relationship will not always be fun, but will be forever rewarding.

This Thanksgiving Eve, I had the opportunity to share a phone call with my mentor, Kevin Bracy, and his mentor, Les Brown. Les was the man who helped open my eyes to what I was truly capable of doing. Kevin was the man who pushed my legs into motion and moving in the right direction, to help those dreams become a reality. Now, I was on the phone with both of them. After that call, I was extremely moved and thankful. Who would have thought that a long-haired kid, putting a third-generation cassette into his beat up old car, would be someday living the dreams that he thought were only a fantasy. Who would have guessed that Les Brown would scream "Shef!" even in my dreams? My momma did; she just knew! ⚑

Eric Brian Robinson
Cheryl W. Robinson

Two the Top Enterprises
PO BOX 182177
Arlington, Texas 76096
817-542-5015 or 214-457-5987
1-(877)-ALWAYZE (259-2993)

Eric Brian Robinson is evolving as one of Dallas/Fort Worth's premier motivational speakers. Robinson is rapidly and innovatively chartering a new course to infuse personal growth and development. Robinson uses a unique style of combining creative forms of communication to deliver his message, "I believe I bring a fresh approach that inspires the hearts and minds of people through skits, drama, and poetry."

Born and raised in Buffalo, New York, Robinson had more than weather to contend with. Growing up in high-rise projects, a troubling family environment, disappointing academic challenges, and teen fatherhood, (which eventually led to single parenting), presented more than his fair share of obstacles. The Johnson C. Smith University graduate refused to allow the adversity he encountered to dictate his future, but to build upon it! The inspirational architect along with his wife, Cheryl, www.cherylwrobinson.com designed the blueprint for Two the Top Enterprises, a motivational company that fosters building positive relationships for prosperous productivity. "When we put single-mindedness into anything, we limit our possibilities." Matthew 18:19 says, "Again I say unto you, That if two of you shall agree on earth as touching anything that they shall ask, it shall be done for them of my Father which is in heaven." In relation the two in our business relates to legitimate relationships be it husband/wife, parent/child, teacher/student, employee/employer etc., supporting each other to reach their highest potential.

The psychology major is definitely shaking things up in the genre of motivational speaking. For more information, check out! www.ericbrianrobinson.com

Cheryl W. Robinson was born in Los Angeles, California and raised in Buffalo, New York where she earned a Bachelor of Arts degree from Medaille College.

Since a young child, Cheryl has always exhibited a passion for writing. The youngest daughter born to a dynamic Baptist Minister whom exemplified tenacity and personified faith, Cheryl never lacked inspiration. She chose writing poetry and essays as her creative outlet. Mrs. Robinson, a Media Communications major writes from the heart and always exhibits spirited candor, phenomenal grace and sometimes amazing wit!

Her work has been featured in several publications and read at many Dallas area venues. In addition her inspirational column may be read online at www. wenetworktx.com. Her gift of messaging through analogies always leaves the reader thinking and always encouraged...

Cheryl is also CEO of Always Encouraging, a division of Two the Top Enterprises that communicates the building of self and relationships through the power of written and spoken word. For more information please visit www.alwaysencouraging.com

The Robinson's reside in Arlington, Texas and proudly share four children. The couple may be reached at:

Two the Top Enterprises
PO BOX 182177
Arlington, Texas 76096
817-542-5015 or 214-457-5987
1-(877)-ALWAYZE (259-2993)

The Significance of Food:
Feeding Your Motivation

"Food is our common ground, a universal experience"
— **James Beard**

America is considered the "land of plenty," especially true when it comes to food and our choices. No doubt we are afforded the opportunity to eat healthily; however, we tend to gravitate towards fast food loaded with saturated fats. Unfortunately, the majority of us tend to do the same with our "life" choices, opting for "processed" substances, which hold no nutritional value, poison our attitudes and our progress. America is also known as "the land of opportunity." Still we choose to live a life of mediocrity. Nonetheless, food is a universal staple that no one can afford to live without. It's even been said that [food] has a language all its own! While the types of food we consume can affect our productivity, attitudes, and life span, so can our choices. We all are privileged, however, to *change… but we must be motivated to do so.* The first challenge arises in recognizing the significance of who we are, why we're here and what we're going to do about it.

Many of us can relate to the phrase, **"You are what you eat!"** This statement can be quite puzzling if one takes it literally. For instance, when you look in the mirror, you don't see yourself as the giant hamburger, large fry, the thick slice of chocolate cake you had for lunch, or the super-sized *diet* Dr. Pepper you washed it all down with! Hmmmn, what if you did? Major advertisers bank on our visual reaction to ads depicting cheese laden double meat patties, double fudge icing, icy-cold beverages…etc., and we respond. At the same time, if you were advertising yourself how would you be depicted? Moreover, there is never a caption that reads:

Warning: 30 minutes after consumption of these foods, you will experience reduced levels of productivity, sleepiness and irritability. More importantly the long-term results of consumption may elevate your blood pressure, cholesterol and shorten longevity.

What are you advertising and what's your disclaimer?

"Tell me what you eat, I'll tell you what you are"
—**Anthelme Brilliant Savarin**

Let's flip the script, many of us have desires, dreams and goals to be or do something in the universe. However, because of our mental diet choices we've slowed down our productivity. By consistently dining on magazines, (adult, comic or otherwise) senseless television shows and negative self-talk we jeopardize, not only our goals but also our vision. Junk **in** equals' junk out! Filling our minds and *bellies* with non-nutritious products does nothing but weaken our productivity, destroying the "big" picture if you will.

Dieters can attest that changing your old eating habits is no easy feat. The most effective way to reaching your personal goal may call for completely changing your diet, but the change must be gradual. On the other hand, you may have already established a few "good" habits that require no change just embellishing. Nonetheless in order to pre-empt failure, you might begin with a "goal" diary. Document your plans for success, devour everything positive, except nothing ala dente. Envision yourself writing that best-selling novel, speaking to that sold out audience or snagging that mega business deal. Make healthy choices that will reflect what you want to be. What's your vision?

"Hunger, one of the few cravings that cannot
be appeased with another solution"
—Irwin Van Grove

We all can relate to hunger pangs, those unmistakable pleas from our stomachs when it craves to be fed. Our stomach communicates to us with growls and rumbles reminding us that it needs to be satisfied. In response, this "signal" causes us to scourer through our kitchen cabinets and refrigerator for anything to satisfy the call. "You're hungry!" and you know exactly what to do to ease the discomfort... EAT!

Let's look at this from a standpoint of satisfying our purpose. If you didn't know, we all were created with a purpose, you should! We were not placed here on earth just to occupy space. How many times have you been told that you've missed your calling, you're in the wrong job, or you're really good at this, why don't you do this for a living? Ironically you've probably asked yourself the same questions, why? It's not like you haven't experienced the "purposed" hunger pangs but because of lack of confidence, fear and sometimes-plain old "hard headedness" you choose to live with the pain. First off you must change your attitude. We know the old cliché, attitude is everything, and it is. Most of us adopt the attitude, it's not my time, or they're just saying that to be nice, or the big one, if I had the money!

The premise for our company "Two the Top" Enterprises, is about relationships. The building and strengthening of relationships between husband/wife, teacher/student or employer/employee, etc. for a positive purpose. The first step is having a positive "attitude". Though sometimes it takes more than a great attitude to propel us into our destiny, we need others. On a more personal note, not long ago, my wife and I attended a networking seminar where we heard a dynamic motivational speaker.

At the end of his presentation he announced that he was looking for Speaker Trainees. My stomach started to growl, but I sucked it up to several unwarranted reasons. The beautiful woman seated next to me, heard the rumbling and stated, "That's you! You need to check it out!" I looked at my wife and nodded my head, but my attitude was that I was willing to go home *hungry*, possibly irritated without as much as a taste-test. Because of "our" relationship, however, my wife had to repeatedly reiterate my purpose and her desire to see me operating within it. Cheryl had to force-feed me the opportunity.

Without that type of encouragement, I would still be starving, snacking on procrastination, denying my calling. Who's holding your spoon, because you're afraid to hold your own? Are those engaged at your dining table feeding your attitude or starving it? In other words, are they saying, "Yeah, you're right, you're not ready!" or are they driving you to a smorgasbord? You decide.

> *"You got to be hungry!"*
> —**Les Brown**

We have all seen the television programs that are pleading for us to help support a malnourished child in a foreign country. We sit and watch often horrified by the images of these children. The children who are closest to death have lost their appetite completely and the hunger pangs have ceased to exist. They are lethargic and without hope and must be forced to eat. Depending on how far the malnutrition has progressed, after receiving enough nutrients, they eventually regain their appetite and resume eating on their own.

Our purpose can be like this as well. If we stop eating or consuming or desiring the things that enable us to grow and mature into what we were placed here to do, we will eventually *lose* our appetites. Like every living entity on earth if you don't eat you will eventually die until your commissioned hunger returns, you may need to be force fed, if you are not strong enough to feed yourself. Bon appetite.

Since I was a little girl, I've always loved to write! I enjoyed writing short- stories; plays, poems but I would keep them to myself. Only a few family members and friends knew of my passion. Then one day a family friend encouraged me to share my writing with someone she knew who could possibly help me develop my skill. So at the age of 16 I gathered up my homemade portfolio and turned it over to a complete stranger for review. Of course, I didn't know what I was doing. I just wanted to share my work and was excited someone might be interested in it. Well, I never saw my portfolio again. I was told it was lost. My spirit was broken and my passion died, or so I thought.

While continuing my education I was always fond of my English classes and a few times I was recognized for my literary style, but I wouldn't allow myself to get excited. I only wrote if asked to do so. As a result I buried my gift. Twenty years later, however, it experienced a resurrection, per se... When I met my husband, like all new relationships we talked about what we liked to do. Surprisingly, I revealed I liked to write. To this very day, I have no idea why I let that secret go! Since then Eric has encouraged me to revive my gift and to pursue my literary dreams. More importantly to write, Write, WRITE!

From that one encouraging conversation, my passion was renewed and now several publications have welcomed my rebirth. I *ACTED* irresponsibly when I turned over my work blindly to an unknown source that could have proved fatal. Some deaths are accidental, or are they? I entrusted my gift to someone who had no regard for its value. Certainly, no one plans to fail- we only fail to plan.

All of us have a natural born appetite- a selective taste, which conforms to our gifts. Those who recognize their palate do not stop to monitor their intake- as they've already set the table with the "appropriate" menu. In essence they already researched what elements will provide them with successful longevity.

Methuselah, the oldest man to live in biblical times, ate, lived and died — unconscious of the blessing of a perfect appetite. Do you think about prosperity and what you need to get there? Or are you a modern day Methuselah? Is your palate purposely representing what you need to do to accomplish your goals, or do you lack motivation, content with eating what's placed before you? Have you decided what sustenance is significantly vital for your purposed survival? Do you need to grocery shop or soul shop? ♠

Eric John Fields

469-569-1503

EF1@hotmail.com

Eric John Fields is the eldest son of John and Mary Fields. He grew up in beautiful East Texas. And after graduating from high school, Eric went on to college and earned an Associate Degree in Mechanics.

However, by age 24, Eric realized that something was missing from his dream, and that caused him a lot of frustration and confusion. He soon realized that his self-worth did not lie in mechanics, so he relocated to Dallas in order to regroup and to discover a new dream.

Eric makes his home in Duncanville, Texas with his wife, Barb and stepson, Cedric. Eric is available to infuse your school, corporate or church group, and can be reached at 469-569-1503, or via e-mail at EF1@hotmail.com.

The Journey

When asked which skills are needed for creating unlimited success, the following are usually mentioned: creativity, communication, principles, goal-seeking, persistence, visualization, decision-making and team building. Individuals who possess or master at least a couple of these, can also achieve unlimited success. I can relate to two of these; 1) principle: a fundamental truth, a rule of conduct and 2) persistence: continuing in the face of opposition, continuing to exist or endure.

I have my father, John Fields, to thank for teaching and instilling principles and the power of persistence within me from a very early age. My father taught me as well as my mother and siblings, how to stay true to your own heart and to never give up on your goals in life.

This chapter was designed with you in mind! The information is simple and life-changing. Let this chapter serve as a motivational and inspirational accumulation of words and allow it to take the limits off what you foresee in your life.

Upon graduating high school, I immediately enrolled at a local college while working nights at an ammunition company. I attended college during the day, and I worked as a machinist at night. And at this particular time in my life, I was not completely settled on what I wanted to do with myself.

My parents let me know that I had to have some type of plan or goal. Thus, I began my journey to secure a degree and stay employed. While doing so, I had taken a triumphant step to achieve my personal dreams. Many people do not fulfill their dreams because they do not even attempt to take any action. I was willing to let go and activate these dreams. My dreams were destined to become a reality.

However, after completing college, there was a layoff at my job, which left me seeking other employment. The area in which I lived was not very developed, and jobs were very scarce. I had my schooling behind me, but was now faced with a different task. I made my way to the unemployment office in my area, but I also went out on my own seeking employment.

I was still unsure and not quite ready to commit to a mechanic position. There just had to be something out there for me, something that would surely captivate me. I had not yet heard back from the unemployment office when a part-time position as a bartender became available to me. Though the position was for Friday and Saturday nights only, I accepted it because bills were still coming in and had to be paid. Now, I just had to convince the owner of the club that I could do a good job. So, I stopped at the library and got a book on "mixing" drinks, and the rest is history. I succeeded at what I had set out to do by having faith in myself. Faith was my first approach to a last resort situation, and it helped me succeed at the task at hand. I continued to exercise the "Power of Principle and Persistence."

The owner of the club was so impressed with me and my attitude to "serve" people that he offered me a position as club manager. This would at least be full-time, and would put much more money in my wilting pockets. I accepted the challenge and with the faith to succeed, I once again put my faith into action. My faith was going to give me success at this position. Little did I know how taxing this work would be on me—physically and mentally, and I rarely had any time for myself. The lifestyle took me much faster than I could have anticipated. Even on my days off, there was still club business that had to be taken care of by me, because I was the manager. There were affairs to be booked, money to be counted, trips to be made to the bank, employees to be managed and paid—it never seemed to end. I became mentally and physically exhausted, and realized that this was not the lifestyle for me.

Therefore, after approximately eight months, I knew I had to give it up. Something had stirred my curiosity at the club. Each time I had to address the crowd this rush would come over me, and I realized I liked that feeling. I was amazed at this observation, but I still had to go.

I moved to Dallas with new hopes and aspirations. The position at the new club had tapped into a new resource for me—the art of public speaking. After settling into the Dallas area, I secured a job within the retail arena in sales. This opened up a whole new world for me. The job gave me the opportunity to showcase myself and to meet a range of interesting people. I became increasingly interested in preparing myself for this new venture. This time I had a burning desire and passion to succeed. I did not wait for any certain contact to happen, and I set no limits!

It is important to know what you want and be clear about it. Wanting something is one thing, working to get it is quite another. To get what you want out of life, in the words of Les Brown, "you've got to be hungry"—for it! You deserve the very best in life, which means more than just having to live with whatever comes along. You have a choice. You can either let things happen or make things happen. I chose to make becoming a motivational speaker a reality in my life.

And once I decided to become a motivational speaker, I decided to join Toastmasters International, which teaches you how to become a more effective communicator. I started attending self-improving seminars, conferences, and lectures. During these times, I took the initiative to introduce myself to people affiliated with the speaking industry.

Les Brown was in Dallas doing a PBS special at KERA television station, and there I met James Parker of James Parker International. And the friendship with James turned into an eight-month, part-time job doing personal leadership development training. This was a great opportunity for me, which allowed me to begin living my dream. The job altered my circumstances and my life. It began to change my life. I started dwelling on the positive things in my life. The picture of my dream started to look clearer to me.

On my job as a salesman, I met my now wife. She also worked at the company where I was employed. We formed a friendship which eventually turned into a dating relationship. She helped me understand what was most important to me, and this also helped to center me. My life was becoming healthy and balanced. And before long, Barb learned how important it was to me, to live my dream, which was to become a professional motivational speaker.

In our fast-paced, high-tech world—opportunities are too often missed to express love for others. But when you evaluate your life, your success should be based on the essential element—Love. And giving love to my wife helped symbolize my ability to experience joy in my life now.

Barb and I are working well together, and things are now coming together for us. And I want to thank her for all of the support and encouragement she has given me, and for making the commitment to be my life partner on this journey. She is also the love of my life as well as my best friend, because she is the "wind beneath my wings."

If I had not taken the initiative, many of the opportunities that came my way, may not have ever been. I am happy to say that my persistence paid off—I stuck to my principles, and now, I am living my dream. Therefore, in order to succeed in any endeavor—the most important factor is YOU. I hope you are following your "blueprints" for success.

"Succeed without limits!"

In closing, I will leave you with this simple acronym: **ERIC FIELDS**.

E—Education is great, and you must be prepared for the opportunity when it is presented. As the saying goes, "It is better to be prepared for an opportunity, than to have an opportunity and not be prepared." Spend time reading books, listening to educational CDs, audio tapes, and videos. Read at least one book a month.

R—Relax to enjoy the journey. Take time to enjoy and have fun along the way. Celebrate all of your accomplishments—you deserve a break. Remember to always have fun achieving your goals.

I—Integrity. Do what you say you are going to do. If you cannot live up to it, let the person know, because your word is your bond. Do not put it out there if you cannot come through. Say what you mean and mean what you say. What you say is who you are.

C—Confidence is just a positive state of mind. When you find yourself losing confidence, remember you have prepared for this moment and everything is working in you to help you reach your goal.

F—Families are who we are after all. They are a looking glass and in the best of cases, they can be a source of energy that can fuel the fire we need for getting the best things we want out of life.

I—Improve yourself. James Allen says in his book, "As A Man Thinketh," people are interested in improving their circumstances, but they are unwilling to improve themselves.

E—Embrace change. Change is a fact of life. And yet, most of us fear and resist change. We want to manifest this moment, a situation, a relationship or an idea, and stay planted in that reality.

L—Listen to a motivational audio daily. Listening to a motivational audio will help you override the negative conversations that take place in your own mind.

D—Discipline is a necessary part of living. The question you must ask yourself is whether you will empower yourself, or allow yourself to be controlled by others.

S—Support: "Support of others"—when you provide something of value to others, you always get more in return. Did you know that one of the keys to achieving success in life has more to do with what you do for others than what you do for yourself? ⬆

Midori Dunn

wewillbefree@sbcglobal.net

(877)617-2996

Midori Dunn is a wife, mother, business owner, author, speaker, and member of Toastmasters. Born and raised in Hawaii, Midori attributes her genuine love for people to her upbringing and to the example set forth by her mom.

Golf, a major part of her life since the age of 5, she played in high school, college, and professionally for 2 ½ years. She traveled throughout the United States and abroad. Through golf, Midori learned the value of character, integrity, and of chasing a dream.

Midori earned her Bachelor's of Business Administration in Marketing and Management from the University of Hawaii at Manoa. She continued her self-education by becoming a student and an active participant of personal development, relationship building, and success principles.

She and her husband Jonathan own a successful and ever-growing Interactive Commerce business. Midori is also the co-owner and co-founder of www. TextToInspire.com. Text to Inspire offers people a way to receive motivational quotes and inspirational words of encouragement on a daily basis through text-messages.

Midori understands the value and importance of a positive and productive attitude, mentorship, effective communication, relationship building, and self-improvement. She has definitely learned that success principles are consistent throughout all facets of life from golf to business to leadership to marriage to parenthood and beyond.

Midori Dunn looks forward to being of service to you, your family, and your organization. Through her life experiences, she unveiled a precious gem of information… you and your dreams are worth the effort. Make every breath count.

Riding the Coaster

Proclaiming Your Birthright

Before we even get started here, I want you to know that you are a winner. You are special and in the famous words of Les Brown, "You have greatness within you." You have everything you need to succeed in life and to live the life you have always dreamed of. God created you in His image and He bestowed upon you such amazing innate abilities. I believe He gave you the power to not only live life, but to create the ideal life for yourself filled with love, joy, peace, happiness, prosperity, accomplishment, and fulfillment. But first, you have to believe that you are worth the effort and I'm here to tell you that YOU ARE. I like what Oprah Winfrey says, "In every aspect of our lives, we are always asking ourselves, how am I of value? What is my worth? Yet I believe that worthiness is our birthright." Worthiness is our birthright, it's YOUR birthright. Proclaim it.

Fleeting Phenomenon

Through experience, I have found this to be true: motivation can be a fleeting phenomenon. One day you have it and the next day it's gone. You look all over for it and for some reason or another, you just can't find it. After a while, you surmise that you'll get it back later. Therefore, for the time being, you feel compelled and justified to sit on the couch and exercise the muscles in your thumb with remote control push-ups. Does this sound familiar? It does to me.

I thought that if I just sat around and waited for it, that motivation would somehow fall into my lap. Let me tell you, it was a huge wake-up call when I realized that it was up to me to make things happen. I couldn't spend my time expecting success to come to me. I had to create an environment where success could flourish. Dexter Yager told me this pearl of wisdom, "Success is the progressive realization of a worthwhile dream."

Realizing Dreams Come True

Motivation stems from the seeds of dreams. Dreams give you the fuel to overcome any obstacle that may come your way. It's the internal desire that you have to make your dreams a reality that gives you the motivation you're looking for. That's why it's extremely vital for you not to let your dreams get lost, stolen, or forgotten.

I believe one of the major pitfalls that we succumb to is letting ourselves lose sight of our dreams. We let our dreams dissipate and dissolve. We just let them float off into the air or sometimes we drop them to the ground and we let other people stomp all over them. What's even worse is that we even let them end up in the Morgue of Forgotten Dreams awaiting burial. I don't want to see that happen and I definitely don't want that to happen to you. Your life has value and meaning and you have the choice to live your dreams. Don't get caught in the pitfall of forgetting about your dreams. Dreams are what make the world go around. If you look around you right now, you will see an array of dreams come true. The book you're holding in your hands right now is a dream come true. What you're reading on this page is a dream of mine come true. If you're sitting down on a chair, couch or bench, you're sitting on someone's dream come true.

Let's not forget this cool and very important fact, YOU are also a dream come true…God's dream come true.

Dodging Curves

Now I know that sometimes life can throw us a few curves. We can all agree on the fact that there are a lot of situations that pop-up unexpectedly in life and can sometimes throw us of track. We all need something we can do to help dodge the curves and keep us focused while we are on our journey towards success. I am going to share with you some of my favorite activities that have helped me on my wonderful journey through life. I do them on a daily basis and I recommend that you do the same. Like Jim Ryan says, "Motivation is what gets you started. Habit is what keeps you going."

Dream-Building

The first thing I would recommend is go dream-building every chance you get. This is a wonderful activity that you can do by yourself and with your family.

Dream-building gives you the opportunity to expand the vision you have in your mind. It allows you to create a clearer picture in your mind's eye of what you would like your lifestyle to be like. Do you remember when you were a child and you believed that you could be anything, do anything, and have anything? You had a zest for life that exemplified a free spirit filled with faith, belief, and unwavering conviction. I want you to feel that way again, so let your imagination run wild and free.

One fun thing you should definitely go out and do is test-drive the car of your dreams. Get a feel for what it's like to sit in the driver's seat and to put your hands on the steering wheel which seems to be molded perfectly to fit your grasp. Reach out to the dashboard and touch all the gadgets that help make the car ride more comfortable. Can you smell that "new car" scent, but more specifically, the scent of YOUR new car? When you turn the ignition on and the engine hums, it sounds like sweet music to your ears. As soon as your foot hits the gas pedal and you put the car in gear, you feel as if you are gliding above the ground. The ride is smooth and effortless and the car handles like a dream, just as you imagined it, only right then at that very moment, you are actually experiencing it first hand. Doesn't it feel wonderful? The best part about it is the car can be yours if you truly want it.

Henry David Thoreau said, "Go confidently in the direction of your dreams. Live the life you've imagined." The fact of the matter is you can pretty much have anything you want in life. The kicker, however, is you've got to know what you really want, you've got to really want it, and you've got to work for it.

Knowing 'Why' Not Only 'How To'

The problem I see with most people and myself included is that we know what to do, but we don't have a strong enough reason 'why' to do it. There isn't a shortage of 'how to' out there. If you watch TV, read the paper, watch movies, surf the Internet, you will find a 'how to' for everything from 'how to lose weight' to 'how to have a successful marriage' to 'how to become a self-made millionaire' and the list goes on and on. Like I said before, there isn't a shortage of 'how to' there is only a shortage of knowing 'why'.

Motivation comes from knowing why you want to do something in the first place. In our Interactive Commerce network marketing business, the first step in our Pattern for Success is to Define Your Dream. Without completing this first step, there would be no reason to move forward. True motivation comes from within. Most, if not all, super achievers have intrinsic motivation. From the depths of their soul, they have a force that drives them to act on their dreams. A clear and distinct picture of what they want to achieve is ingrained in their subconscious mind. Their desire and passion cause them to be men and women of steadfast resolve and unbendable perseverance. They will not rest until their thirst is quenched with achievement, triumph, and victory. I would bet top dollar that super achievers not only understand the benefits and power of dream–building, but they also do it on a consistent basis.

Reading

Another beneficial activity you can do is read at least one to two chapters a day from a motivational book. I usually read when I get up in the morning because I enjoy starting my day off with a smile and a positive attitude. I also read before I go to bed at night because this gives me a chance to inundate my mind with positive thoughts and I like to fall asleep with visions of creating a better life for myself and my family. I love reading motivational books because it gives me another perspective on life. I get to learn from the experiences of highly successful people and you can do the same, too. What took these people years to learn, struggle through, and figure out, we can read about in a few minutes and use their wisdom to improve ourselves and our lives.

Studying

By the looks of it, I would say that you are already ahead of the game because you're reading this motivational book right now. I want to take you one step further and share with you a powerful piece of advice that my mentor Kevin Bracy taught me. Don't just read the words on the page, STUDY them. Understand the principles behind the stories and implement them into your own life. Mike Murdock says, "The difference between prosperity and poverty is wisdom. Wisdom comes from two places – mistakes and mentors." I would encourage you to let the authors of these motivational books become your "study from" mentors. Words are powerful forces and they can help motivate you to action. You can learn from the mistakes of other people and use their wisdom to create better habits in your life that will help you achieve the success you're striving for.

Listening

Another powerful thing that you can do to motivate yourself on a daily basis is to listen to inspirational audios. The best place for doing this is while you're driving. You can turn your car into a University on wheels. I guarantee it will be an education that you can put to good use. You will find it easier to deal with any traffic you encounter and your daily commute will fly by because your attention is focused on something positive and thought-provoking. Oprah Winfrey puts it profoundly, "If you want your life to be more rewarding, you have to change the way you think." Listening to inspirational audios can help you do just that.

Taking Time

If you'd like another source of motivation, I would recommend
that you take time to really figure out what you love to do. One of
my passions in life is dancing. Anyone who knows me knows that I
love to dance. Dancing allows me to break free of my worries and it
gives me a chance to drift off into a world of my own. I find it to be
invigorating and intoxicating. When I'm dancing, my heart beats faster
and I get chicken skin because I am doing something that I love.

I believe we need more of that in our lives, pure unadulterated passion.

The Bible says in Ecclesiastes 3:1-8 that there is a time for everything.

Take Time:
Take time to think – It is the source of all power.
Take time to read – It is the fountain of wisdom.
Take time to play – It is the source of perpetual youth.
Take time to be quiet – It is the opportunity to seek God.
Take time to be aware – It is the opportunity to help others.
Take time to love and be loved – It is God's greatest gift.
Take time to laugh – It is the music of the soul.
Take time to be friendly – It is the road to happiness.
Take time to dream – It is what the future is made of.
Take time to pray – It is the greatest power on earth.
Take time to give – It is too short a day to be selfish.
Take time to work – It is the price of success.

Riding the Coaster

In moments of doubt, remind yourself that you are worthy. I want you
to know in your heart of hearts that you are important and that your
existence on this Earth is meaningful and valuable. You are worthy to
live the life of your dreams and I would encourage you to chase after
them with full force and awe-inspiring tenacity.

I want you to know that I believe in you and in your dreams. I want
all the best for you and your family. Always stay in the pursuit of your

dreams because that's where you'll find success. The journey we call life is meant to be a roller coaster ride filled with steep ups and downs and sometimes nauseating twists and turns, but that's what makes the journey fun, exciting, and worthwhile. Commit to memory and action the following quote written by an unknown author, "Life is not a journey to the grave with the intention of arriving safely in a pretty and well-preserved body, but rather sliding in sideways, thoroughly used up, totally worn out and proclaiming, 'WOW! What a ride!'" ⬆

Steve Sapato

(309) 797-6711

steve@stevesapato.com

www.stevesapato.com

Steve has been about the exciting business of changing lives for over 15 years. As a professional speaker and humorist Steve has spoken for numerous Fortune 500 Companies. As an entrepreneur for over 40 years he has owned and operated several businesses and currently owns and operates InterActive Marketing, a breakthrough Internet Marketing Company; Sapato Residential Real Estate Appraisals; The Boulevard reception and meeting hall; and InterActive Seminars, all located out of the Quad-City area in Moline, Illinois and Davenport, Iowa.

His topics cover areas of Customer Service; Goal Setting and Motivation; Attitude Development; Wealth Development; Business Start-Ups; Humorous Seminars and Fun Auctioneering for fund raisers and include titles as Laughing Your Way to a Better Relationship; Living, Laughing, Learning and Loving; Live Your Way to the Top; Your Belief Becomes Your Reality; He Said, She Heard; Peep Over The Pail (to your amazing future); and many more.

Steve understands the challenges of communication between generations, men and women, parents and children, as well as the need for clarity in all areas of communication.

If you are looking for a fun and fantastic seminar that teaches and trains your people then Steve is the person to call.

You can reach Steve through his office at (309) 797-6711, by his eddress at steve@stevesapato.com or his web-site: www.stevesapato.com

This One's For ME!

For all who come to this happy place. Welcome!
—**Walt Disney**

You have heard the phrase "This one's for you" murmured and shouted by many people. Rocky shouted "Yo! Adrian! I did it!" and what all of these people are saying is that they needed motivation from someone else to make their dream come true.

How about you? Do you need some outside motivation to make your dreams come true? Do you need someone out there to be proud of you in order to put your best foot forward? Do you need someone to stand over you to make it all happen for you?

Because right now I want you to say out loud 'THIS ONE'S FOR ME!'. Stop! Don't go any further in this chapter until you say it. Now carefully, with deliberate thought, say this out loud, THIS ONE IS FOR ME!

Did you do it? For most of us, we simply cannot do that. It's embarrassing. It's silly. It's not necessary.

But let me ask you this, if what you are doing is working so well, why are you reading this book? You are looking for more. You are looking for something to be different in your life. You are looking for the secret of what can change who you are so that you can become who you need to be in order to make your dreams come true.

You don't live life as it is, you live life as you are."
—Les Brown

Kevin Bracy's motto is "Brace Yourself" and that's what I want you to do as you read this chapter. Brace yourself for a new you. Brace yourself for a major change coming your way. Brace yourself so that you will be OPEN to what you will need to do, what you must do, what you should do in order to make this change a reality for your life.

Say this again, THIS ONE IS FOR ME! Say it every day. Say it when you are doubting your path. Say it when you aren't certain what to do and the answer will come with clarity. Not, what would others do. Not, what will others think of me. Not, I can't do this. But ask yourself every time, **IF** this one is for me, what do I really want.

Have you asked yourself that before? Here's why you are reading this chapter. What can you learn that will help you get something that you currently do not have? What will you learn that will help you become what you want to become? What will you learn that will help you do what you have not done?

So our first question for you is, DO YOU KNOW WHAT YOU WAN'T TO HAVE, DO, BE, or BECOME?

Most of us don't. In one of my most recent seminars I asked this question of my audience, which was made up of managers and supervisors of several major corporations; How many of you would like to be happier, healthier, have better relationships and/or make more money?

I am asking you that right now? Would you like to be happier than you are today? Be healthier than you are today? Have better relationships than you have today? And/or make more money than you are today?

Did you answer Yes to one, two, three, or all four of these questions?

And if you answered yes to any of those, would you be willing to undertake a task that will lead you to all of those results?

Authors and speakers Zig Ziglar, Brian Tracy, Mark McCormack and me,Steve Sapato, all use the Harvard study that was conducted between 1979 and 1989. The graduates of the Harvard MBA program were asked how many of them had set clear written goals and had made plans to accomplish them.

Only three (3%) percent of the graduates had written goals and plans. Thirteen (13%) percent had goals but they were not in writing. Eighty-four (84%) percent had no specific goals at all other than graduating from school and enjoying their summer.

Ten years later, in 1989, those same people were interviewed and it was found that the thirteen (13%) percent who had goals but that were not written down were earning, on average, twice as much as the eighty-four (84%) percent who had no goals. But most surprisingly, it was found that the three (3%) percent who had the clear, written goals were earning, on average, ten times as much as the other ninety-seven (97%) combined!

They also learned that the three (3%) percent were, on average, happier, healthier, and had longer lasting relationships.

So now I will ask you again—would you like to be happier, healthier, have better relationships and/or make more money than you are today? And are you willing to undertake the steps that will help you accomplish that?

A monastery was perched high upon a cliff and the only access to reach it was by way of riding in a basket which several monks had hauled to the top. Obviously, the ride over the rocky jagged terrain was steep, and in a wicker basket, terrifying to all but the naively fearless. One visitor, however, got exceedingly nervous. Roughly halfway up he saw that the rope by which they were being hauled, was rather frayed and splitting. Shaking in his boots but unable to move, he frantically asked the monk who was seated next to him how often they changed the rope.

Thinking for a moment, the monk answered, "Whenever it breaks."

Is that how you are living your life? We don't fix what ain't broke. And if we are doing "OK" then our lives are not broken. If you are like your neighbors then all it takes is to pay your bills and buy a few things you really want and you are "happy". But you must not be content if you are reading this. You are looking for more.

You are reading this because what you are currently doing is not working as well as you had hoped. You have now learned that one giant step to helping you achieve the life you desire over the life you have is by setting, planning and working toward specific goals in your life. So the first baby step you need to take is to establish what goals you want to achieve for your life.

Here's where your life starts to change…

Have you ever REALLY thought about what you want in life?

Because when I ask most people they cannot write down more than 20 things they want in their life. Can you write down things you want to have, do, be, or become? Have you ever written down how much money you want to make every year, year after year?

Most of us have talked about it. Some of us even dream about it. That usually happens when the lottery reaches one hundred million dollars. I joke that I buy lottery tickets when it reaches that huge number and not before because I couldn't use one million or ten million dollars. That it's not enough to make me stop and buy a ticket. But then we talk about what we would do IF we won the lottery. Have you ever thought about what you would do if you won the lottery? My guess is, you have, because you have a dream, you have a desire, you want more and that's why you ARE reading this right now.

But…we don't believe. Most people cannot write down 100 things they want because they don't BELIEVE they can achieve them. You know you want things but you don't REALLY want them. You certainly aren't going to write down something you are never going to get are you?

So let's start with some basics. You now are on the track to realize your dreams, but what dreams do you WANT?

And before you proceed do you know there is a right way and a wrong way to write things down or say them?

For instance, everyone understands the basic differences between some phrases. An example of this is the phrasing differences between 'your beauty is timeless' rather than saying 'your face could stop a clock'.

But did you know that your mind cannot understand negatives? We spend hours of time, effort, and energy trying to defeat our own demons. Overweight, underweight, lack of exercise, self-doubts and on and on. But think of this. When we often are trying to diet we say to ourselves, "I am not going to eat..." and then we name what it is we aren't going to eat. Chocloate, gravy, sweets, carbs, whatever. But your mind does not understand that phrasing.

Let me show you a different way that occurs. Don't think of a big grey elephant.

What did you just think of? Yup, a big grey elephant. Now if you are REALLY sharp and trying to fool yourself you will say, no I thought of a pink flamingo or something else. Here's how that process happened. You first thought of the elephant then you CONSCIOUSLY changed your thought to think of something else.

But you normally do not do that. If you say, "I am not going to eat apple pie today" then all day long you have a craving for apple pie! No chocolate for a month? Chocolate cravings. I hate being fat simply transcribes into your subconscious as I'm fat.

So how you write your goals is CRITICAL to your success. Write your goals in the present tense. For instance, not "I'm going to weigh 210 lbs" but "I weigh 210 lbs."

Not "I want to have a 2007 Plymouth Prowler" but "I own a 2007 Plymouth Prowler". Or "I own my own home, that is 2,300 sq.ft. and has four bedrooms, 3 baths, with a finished basement with a recroom, bedroom, bath and a pool table, foosball table and air hockey. My back yard has a four season porch, a deck, hot tub, in-ground swimming pool and a playground for my kids."

Smaller goals can have specific dates attached to them, "On December 12th, 2006 I am buying tickets to go to London in the summer of

2007." On March 15th, I am buying a 2.2 cubic foot microwave oven from my own online business for my kitchen at a cost of $220.00."

So now it's your turn. Go grab the writing tablet that is hidden in your desk drawer and start writing. Write down everything that comes to your mind. Everything that you want. Everything you want to become. Every place you want to go.

An example of that might be: I am going to go to—Hawaii, Las Vegas, Alberta, London, Peoria. You see, they don't have to be BIG goals. Just the things YOU want.

Take that tablet out NOW and as you finish reading this book you will discover that you have opened an imagination that may never settle for anything again. You have STARTED your incredible journey toward your dreams.

This dream is for me! Say it as you write each dream. "THIS DREAM IS FOR ME!" Say it out loud. Don't let what others think of you as you say this out loud stop you from your dreams!

Ask yourself this question… how do you want to be remembered? Do you remember your Grandfather? Grandmother? Great Grandfather or Grandmother? Do you think that Donald Trumps children, grandchildren or great grandchildren will have trouble knowing who he was? How about Ray Kroc's family? Oh! Some of you don't even know who Ray Kroc is. He is the man who started McDonalds franchising. Every single time his great-great grandchildren travel down the road they are thankful he had vision, set goals and had one great life. How about Colonel Sanders from Kentucky Fried Chicken? Or Wal-Mart's Sam Walton?

Am I saying you can have that kind of lifestyle? Nope. But I am saying, now, that you have the OPPORTUNITY for that kind of life. Maybe you have never had that opportunity before. Maybe you never want that kind of lifestyle. But NOW, with just what you have learned already, you have opened your mind to new visions, dreams and possibilities.

Are you working on your GOALS? Are you willing to list those goals? Are you willing to put a plan together to help you achieve those goals?

This book is titled A MASSIVE DOSE OF MOTIVATION and I hope that you are learning what MOTIVATES you! What drives you? What will make you greater than you are?

Do you understand what it will take for you to overcome who you ARE to become who you WILL BE?

Do you understand this will be an amazing struggle that will require constant motivation. Constant input. Constant pressure from you or what motivates you?

> *You change your life when you change your mind*
> **—Jim Stovall**

And there are three things that will help you move forward. In all of my motivational seminars I touch on these three things. Because you will be exactly the same person tomorrow as you are today except for these three things: the books you read; the cd's you listen to; and the people you associate with.

You will learn from those things HOW you need to proceed in your life? What you will need to do. What PLAN you will want or need to follow.

Have you ever tried to do something you have never done before? Is it easy? Yes and no, right? Because if there is someone SHOWING you how to do that thing you have never done before it is easy. That person could be called a MENTOR. But if you have never done it before and there are no mentors available it is much harder to do.

> *A purpose is a goal, a plan is a way to get there.*
> **—Zach Sapato**

So your next step will be HOW. How will you accomplish your goals? How will you move forward toward your destiny?

You will find your how when you have enough reasons. I have heard it said that the HOW doesn't matter until you know WHY?

People who know HOW work for the people who know WHY.

Do you have your reason why yet? Have you started writing your goals as you have been reading? Once you start and let your mind experience the freedom of simply listing ALL things you might want without limitations, without judging those choices you will be amazed how you will feel. How you will smile more, laugh more, love more because you will have more to live, laugh and smile about.

When you share those WHY's with your significant other or with someone who WANTS to help you achieve those dreams, your life will change. Your attitude will improve. You will see others change because they will see you change.

So let's go back to the beginning. What is your reason for reading this book? What is it you are looking for? And what are you willing to do to change your life?

Are you willing to write down 100 goals and to spend a significant amount of time discovering those dreams?

Are you willing to put together a photo album representing many of those dreams and leave it on your coffee table or end table as a constant reminder?

Are you willing to read other books, listen to other tapes, and meet with NEW people who can help you achieve those goals through designing a PLAN for your life?

Because you will need to remember this: SNIOP

Susceptible to the Negative Input of Other People

You and I are all susceptible to that negativity. I will guarantee you one thing, that as soon as you start this journey, there will be people in your life; friends, family, loved ones who will try to destroy your dreams. Many of them not on purpose. But you have felt that before. "You can't do that." "Why would you want that? " No one in this family has ever…" "Why can't you just be happy with what you have?"

And you may have never tried to break out of your situation. Have you ever heard of the trained fleas at the circus? How do you train a flea you are asking? Simple. You put the fleas in a bottle with a cap and as you watch, the fleas will bounce up and into that lid over and over again. Until one day, you look, and the fleas no longer reach the top. And then soon you can take the lid off of that bottle and the fleas will never jump out again. WHY? They are trained by experience not to jump that high again.

We are trained that way. When you were a child you had great expectations, huge dreams and an attitude of I CAN DO ANYTHING. Where did that go? Why don't we have that any more?

We were trained where our "lid" was. We were taught by schooling to reach only so high. We were taught by events not to hit our heads on that "lid". I have a son who loved drawing. Was he great at it? I will never know because in junior high school, one of his teachers simply said, "you should not pursue art. You aren't very good at it." And he almost never drew again.

We have all had teachers, friends, family who didn't mean to crush our dreams but have said something similar.

But the message from God is that you are worthy. Worthy of all you can discover. Worthy of all you want. Worthy of dreaming and achieving and accomplishing. Worthy of teaching others that they are worthy.

Because the truth is you CAN accomplish your dreams. You CAN enjoy a better life. You can be who you want to be.

THIS ONE IS FOR ME! is what your motto should be from this day on. Say it again, out loud, with conviction because YOU ARE WORTH IT!

THIS ONE IS FOR ME!

From this day on you can create your own MASSIVE DOSE OF MOTIVATION every time you need it!

If you ever see me at an airport, or in a seminar, please feel comfortable walking up to me and saying "THIS ONE IS FOR ME!" We will laugh and meet and we will both know that you are on your journey to success! ♠

Valerie L. Hawes

Channing Group, LLC

P.O. Box 32066

Columbus, Ohio 43232

614.738.3938 phone

ChanningGroup@aol.com

Valerie L. Hawes is a motivational speaker and professional development trainer educating and entertaining adults and youth to pursue their dreams no matter what!

Valerie is CEO of her own consulting firm, Channing Group, LLC. The firm provides coaching and custom designs training workshops based on organizational and/ or individual needs. Since 2003, Valerie has worked as an Independent Contract Speaker with Monster's Making It Count Programs. She delivers three (3) of the company's 50-minute educational programs and has reached more than 32,000 students throughout the Mid-west region of the United States.

Valerie holds a Bachelors Degree in Social Psychology from Park University and is currently working on her Masters of Science Administration Degree from Central Michigan University. She resides in Columbus, Ohio and is the proud parent of a teenage son, Channing. In addition, Valerie is a co-founder and organizer for the Elite Basketball Club, an organization designed to instruct, develop, and groom young athletes for competitive basketball.

For more information regarding the Channing Group, LLC or to inquire about Valerie's availability to speak for your organization, conference, campus, church, retreats or book club meeting, please contact Valerie at the following address:

Valerie L. Hawes
Channing Group, LLC
P.O. Box 32066
Columbus, Ohio 43232
614.738.3938 phone
ChanningGroup@aol.com

Recognize Your Significance

How can you make wise decisions and choices if you do not understand why you want what you want? What makes you tick? What motivates you? What are you passionate about? You see, a lack of awareness will cause us to shut down. When we are unable to answer these questions, we are susceptible to depression (in other words, shutting down). Knowing these answers allows us to see our true value and significance in the world. That's all any of us really want in life as humans. We need to feel validated. I truly believe that recognizing our significance in the world is a key ingredient to being motivated personally and professionally. It spills over into every aspect of our lives.

We don't always recognize those who live their lives daily with a feeling of insignificance. This is because so many of us walk around wearing disguises or masks of confidence, competence, and invincibility. But the truth will always rear its head in some fashion— if you are paying attention. Most people in the midst of upheaval almost automatically retreat in some way. Some people withdraw into unhealthy habits: sleeping too much or not enough, drinking to excess, eating too much or too little, taking recreational drugs, and so on. There are many ways to flee from the realities of life and still give an outward appearance of participating.

For years, I lived my life just existing. I walked through life doing and believing what I had been taught by my parents, never recognizing my own dreams or significance in this world. When you are too busy listening and following others rather than following your own path, turmoil shows up quite often. These chaotic situations will leave you feeling confused and victimized. These feelings constantly overwhelmed my mind. As far as I was concerned, there was no true significance for my life. While God is using this time as a "wake up call" to His plan, the adversary will try to use these moments of weakness to destroy your mind in hopes to destroy your destiny.

After only 8 months of marriage, I found myself in the middle of a tumultuous divorce. I thought to myself, "How did I get here? I'm so embarrassed. This is not how I planned it. How could he do this to me? Why doesn't he want me anymore? What will I do now?" I didn't believe this at the time, but now I know that everything happens for a reason. Nothing happens in your life coincidentally. God has a purpose and a plan for each of us. He will use any situation and whomever He needs, to get you on the right path. For some of us, it takes longer than others. Some of us (like me) need to be completely shaken in order to sit up and pay attention to life.

For months, fear and anxiety dominated my every thought. I retreated in almost every way imaginable. When I was not in the bed sleeping my life away, near a breakdown, I was intent on pretending that my life was just fine to the outside world. In public, I wore a "mask" of confidence and competence. The mask typically consisted of the finest clothes and a completely made-up face. Flawless and fierce on the outside. However, on the inside, I was filled with apprehension and self-loathing. I could not have explained that to you then. See, I thought I was a victim of perpetual abandonment.

I later realized, once I found peace and safety in my life, that I had also been a victim of myself! I chose to be in that relationship. I gave him permission to mistreat me because subconsciously I felt defective. I felt so out of place in the world. When I interacted with others, I was sure that they knew exactly what they were doing, but that I was only faking it. I did not feel competent. In an effort to overcome this feeling of inadequacy, I decided to continue my education with hopes that obtaining a degree would make me appear more credible and competent.

One day, a friend gave me a book that changed my life. The book was called *One Day My Soul Opened Up*, written by Iyanla Vanzant, a famous inspirational speaker and life coach. The book is a forty-day program of inspiration and motivation designed to help improve emotional and spiritual health. It was not until completion of that book that I realized that I did not have to walk through life just existing but that I could decide to live. I learned that living and existing is not the same thing. This revelation marked the beginning of awareness for me. I started to become more alert to ways that might help me stop the terrifying cycle of breaking apart, trying to put myself back together again, and then existing in a climate of fear and apprehension that would inevitably lead me to another breakdown.

How many people do you know are faking their way through life? Are you? Awareness means understanding what is happening in your life. The art of making choices that create a real, loving, and self-accepting existence is not always taught in school or even by parents. Learning how to recognize the stress factors in your life, and then reacting in a healthy and appropriate way can be difficult for people who have the habit of retreating and faking. I've got wonderful news for you! Life can be grand! It can be whatever you want it to be. It may be okay to "fake it" for a while, but don't make a career of it. Some say, "fake it, until you make," but that only works for a short while. Make sure that you are executing an effective development plan to ensure that what you want to happen in your life does happen.

We are often painfully aware of our shortcomings and oblivious to our best qualities. Becoming aware in a positive and healthy way will help you begin to understand and accept that you are human with all the mistakes and triumphs that accompany the miracle of your existence. If you allow yourself to be fully human, you will become more self-accepting and loving even when you are faced with challenges.

For me, being aware means recognizing the possibilities of what I have to offer the world. Being aware means there is hope. I found that as my ability to be a consciously aware person increased, I found new pleasure in the world around me. It was difficult and it did not happen overnight.

Here are some tips to help you recognize your true significance in life:

Identify your passion.

Your passion will reveal your true significance in life. I believe that God uses our passion to confirm His true purpose for creating us. There is a void in the world that we were sent on earth to fill. Pay attention to your passion. Embrace it. Pursue it. It is the key to true happiness!

Affirm yourself daily.

You may not have the privilege of a cheerleading squad at your front door to "pump you up" with a daily pep rally. Most of do not have this luxury. Some days no one will be around to affirm you. Be your own best cheerleader. Make a list of your talents and gifts. Pat yourself on the back and give yourself a big hug, even if no one else is around to do it for you! You are the only you there is! Everything you need to survive already lives within you. So, show yourself some love. You deserve it!

Establish goals for yourself.

Decide what you want from your life. What do you hope to accomplish? What do want to do? Where do want to be in five years? Ten years? Twenty-five years? Then determine a plan that is measurable, with action steps that are realistic to ensure your success.

Read inspirational and/or self development materials daily.

It is important to nurture our minds, and our spirits daily. Read materials that will keep you uplifted and focused. This will continue to motivate you to pursue your dreams and goals

Take a class.

We should always be open to learning new things. This allows our minds to grow, while keeping us young at heart. I don't care what type of class you decide to take. It could be a professional development class, a literature class, a knitting class, or a tango class. Be open to new things. You may find opportunities to share your passion and talents in places that you least expect. You may even meet someone who can help you achieve your goals.

Meditate daily.
Spend time in quiet. This allows us to become more centered. Hear from God. Sometimes we miss what He wants us to know because there are too many distractions in the way. Reflect on your goals and affirm yourself during this time as well.

Journal daily.
Take time to write your thoughts, dreams, passion, affirmations, and goals daily. When we put these things on paper it almost forces them to manifest. It becomes a contract with yourself.

Find a Mentor.
Find someone who is successfully doing exactly what it is that you want to do. Make contact with them. Become their friend and/or protégé. Learn from the best. Learn how they became successful by asking for their "plan of action" as well as learning about their failures.

Find an accountability partner.
This is a like-minded individual who is on the same path as you. This person will help you to stay focused, and you will do the same for them. "Birds of a feather flock together." It's true!

Pray.
Pray for direction. Pray for strength. Pray for confidence. Pray for the right friends and mentors. Pray for everything!

As I grew in self-awareness, I better understood why I felt what I felt about myself, and my place in this world. I also recognized why I behaved as I had in the past. That understanding then gave me the opportunity and freedom to change and create the life I desired. Without fully recognizing your significance in life, self-awareness becomes impossible. Iyanla Vanzant's book made a deposit in me that I still withdraw from all of the time.

I have finally found my place in the world—the true significance of my life. I currently work as a motivational speaker and trainer, inspiring people to reach their full potential in life. I am a survivor and strive to share my testimony with others who may have experienced despair in their own life. Every experience holds within it a lesson. This is the message I give to you. ⬆

Johnny Wimbrey

Wimbrey Training Systems

1-800-535-7851

www.JohnnyWimbrey.com

The young, dynamic, master motivator known nationally for his record breaking achievements, Johnny Wimbrey trains and encourages thousands through seminars and events throughout the world. His inspirational story of overcoming life's adversities has empowered masses for greatness. Author of, "From the Hood to Doing Good," Wimbrey is marked with life memories of living in a battered women's shelter to growing up on the hard-core streets as a young drug dealer. After several near death experiences Wimbrey decided it was time to flip the switch and refused to let his past determine his future.

At the age of twenty, Wimbrey became a temporary licensed insurance agent with no experience, and within 6 months of being in the insurance industry, he received recognition as a top fifty producer in a national marketing agency. In less than a two-year period, moving from senior agent, to district manager, to regional manager, on to regional vice president overseeing the states of Texas and Oklahoma, Wimbrey found himself in the position of training experienced regional managers to recruit, to manage, and to teach sales development skills for well-known national agencies.

After recognizing the high demand for his services, Wimbrey decided to use his skills for a higher purpose. His passion is to create success stories by helping others experience financial, spiritual, and emotional wealth. Wimbrey has been interviewed on national radio talk shows and television networks as a young success story. Wimbrey has been featured as the special guest speaker for ZIG ZIGLAR TRAINING SYSTEMS, and has shared the stage with other world famous speakers like Les Brown, Bill Bailey, and Jim Rohn.

Johnny's message is to expose the reality, "Your past doesn't determine your future and if I can do it, anyone can." Johnny is a professional member of the National Speakers Association.

Let's WIN BIG together,
Johnny Wimbrey
www.JohnnyWimbrey.com

The Psychology of Winning!

Almost all situations have an easy way out, but the prize for the race is not always given to the quick; instead, it is given to the one who perseveres and finishes the race. Winners understand that through the thick and thin, we must win! Failure is not an option for winners. They say winners never quit. I can guarantee you a quitter will never be a winner!

A true winner also understands the importance of surrounding himself or herself with other winners. I have made it a personal goal in my life to constantly introduce myself to, and continuously surround myself with, people who stretch me. All winners understand that you must get out of your comfort zone. You can't learn how to swim in shallow waters. Don't be afraid of the deep. It's hard to move to a higher level if everyone around you is beneath you or on the same level as you. I don't mean beneath you as in you are better as a person than they are, because we know that we are ALL created equally. What I mean is, for example, if you want to become an executive at your job, then you need to expose yourself to the mentality of an executive. There are a lot of people who are, or have been, where you are trying to go. You cannot follow a parked car. Hang around winners and you will become a winner too!

The Importance of Having Mentors

Winners understand and value the importance of having mentors. I have found that in many cases people use the word "mentor" very loosely. A mentor, first of all, is someone that you know personally. You may admire someone on TV, but he or she is not your mentor unless you have access to him or her. You choose your mentor; your mentor does not choose you. You may be approached by someone who wants to put you under his or her wing and guide you, but until you choose to go, he or she is not your mentor. In addition, your mentor must accept the role, or he or she is not a mentor. A mentor should be able to correct you on the spot; you submit immediately and take heed of his or her direction. This is why you choose your mentor. Because the moment you begin to unwillingly receive advice, correction, or even open rebuke, then he or she is no longer your mentor.

Synonyms for the word mentor: Teacher, Adviser, Tutor, Counselor, Guru, Guide. Webster's dictionary defines the mentor as "A trusted counselor or guide."

In order to have a mentor, you must be a protègè!

Synonyms and definition of the word protègè: dependent, student, disciple, one who accepts the charge.

You can have different mentors for different areas of your life. For example, you may have a physical mentor, a spiritual mentor, and a financial mentor. It's great if all of these are the same person, but it's not necessary.

How Do You Choose a Mentor?

1. He/she has something that you would also like to have or experience. Example: You play the saxophone and he/she is very good with the sax.

2. He/she agrees to mentor you.

3. He/she must be someone who can tell you NO!

4. He/she has a lifestyle you respect in every facet.

5. He/she must be someone that you can be honest with, no matter what!

> *In the multitude of counselors there is safety.*
> —**King Solomon**

Mentors' jobs are to protect us. That's why it's very important that we be open and honest with them so they can tell, show, and give us everything we need that is in our best interests. True mentors will tell us what we need to hear, instead of what we want to hear.

Great mentors will inspect what they expect. In other words, they won't just tell us what to do; they will follow up or make sure we report our results. Mentors are not dictators but advisors who want us to succeed without sacrificing our integrity. Great mentors will never ask us to compromise good character to get to the top.

A great financial mentor will show you how to master your money, instead of your money mastering you. When your money tells you what to do, you are in trouble, but when you can tell your money what to do, you can and will experience true wealth.

I once read that open rebuke is better than hidden love. A great mentor understands that he or she must tell it to you like it is.

A great winner is also a great protégè who will apply the advice from the mentor that he or she chose. A mentor has every right to terminate a relationship with a rebellious protégè. Likewise, the protégè has every right to terminate a relationship with his or her mentor. Keep in mind, if you find yourself jumping from mentor to mentor because they are not what you expected them to be, chances are they are not the ones with the problems.

I will tell you from experience that there are plenty of times I have gotten my feelings hurt by my mentors, but remember, I chose them. Winners are not afraid of constructive criticism and understand that it takes iron to sharpen iron.

My wife Crystal and I are very blessed to have incredible marital mentors, Eben and Sara Conner, who hold us accountable to each other. We chose them; they did not choose us. They have counseled us on several occasions. I must admit that when I know I am right, I am very quick to call them to referee when Crystal and I are having intense fellowships (arguments). I do confess that the majority of the times I call them in so Crystal can get help (because I am right). Usually, I end up being the one getting the most help.

Did you know that it is possible to deceive yourself? Deception would not be deception if it were obvious! You can be off track and not know it. And without correct navigation you will eventually crash.

Crystal and I know that Eben and Sara want us to win in every facet of our lives. And since they have our best interests at heart, we agree to submit to their wisdom. Wisdom is the application of knowledge. So when they share their knowledge, as their protègès we must apply their instructions, regardless of who is at fault.

A winner knows when to swallow his or her pride in order to resolve a higher cause and/or purpose. Winners understand that it is impossible to win by themselves.

Winners MUST Win!

Winners don't see success as an option; we see it as something that we must have. Average people want to win, but winners must win. While the majority of the world is talking about what they want to happen, the mentality of the winner is focused on what must happen. As a winner, you must be able to convert every one of your wants to your musts. When you want something, it's optional. But when you must have something, it's non-negotiable. Everyone wants to be successful; only a very few must be successful.

So how do you turn your wants into your musts? I've done seminars across the nation on this topic. And when I ask the audience to give me a list of things that are a must in their lives, here are some of the common answers that I get.

THINGS PEOPLE MUST HAVE OR DO
be at work on time
pay bills on time
eat
bathe
buy groceries
pay taxes

Here is a common list of answers that I get when I ask for things they want.

THINGS PEOPLE WANT TO HAVE OR DO
eat healthy
exercise
go on vacation
pray every day
give to charity
spend more time with the family

OK, by now you should get the point. The only difference between the things that you must have or do and the things that you want to have or do is you. Your attitude determines your ability to succeed.

Typically, the things that most people see as a must are tied to negative consequences. For example, if you don't eat, you starve. Or if you don't show up for work on time, you will get fired. In other words, most people are programmed to perform in order to prevent immediate negative reactions. You have a why for all your musts.

On the other hand, there are the few who are driven by the thrill of success. These individuals understand that they must do today what others don't, to have tomorrow what others won't. These are the ones who have the ability to make things happen, and who are self-disciplined. It is very important to have a reason, or a why, for everything that you want.

EXAMPLE I "must" be successful because I "want" to leave an inheritance for my children's children.

When you find your why in everything that you want and become passionate with a burning desire for the end result, your wants will become musts. Therefore, you must find your why for all of your wants.

Wants + Whys = Musts

I MUST eat healthy to live longer.
I MUST exercise for energy and for good health.
I MUST go on vacation because I work hard.
I MUST pray every day to stay spiritually strong.
I MUST give to charity to save lives.
I MUST spend more time with my family to show my love.

My cause is bigger than me, and because my wants have whys that are much more important than selfish desires, I am willing to fight for the end result. You must be willing to fight for the cause of your wants. It's hard to fight for something without a cause, so connect all of your wants to all of your whys so that all of your dreams will come to fruition.

To receive a FREE gift from Johnny Wimbrey go to www. JohnnyWimbrey.com and join his FREE Ezine! To have Johnny Wimbrey speak at your next event please contact Wimbrey Training Systems at 1-800-535-7851 or visit www.JohnnyWimbrey.com ⬥

82

Norma Bryant Howard

E-mail: nhoward926@insightbb.com

A native of Louisville, Kentucky, Norma honed her skills in public speaking, which contributed to her developing and conducting workshops and speeches on business fashion, motivation, self esteem and goal setting. She received her B.A. Degree from Kentucky State University, a Post Baccalaureate Degree in Elementary Education and a Masters Degree in Elementary Education from the University of Louisville.

Norma has conducted many Professional Image Seminars which have focused on college seniors, young executives, and both men and women in the Welfare-to-Work Program where she has motivated and inspired many individuals to move up to the next level in life. Other speaking engagements include being the keynoter for the Kentucky Real Estate Exchangers, Jefferson County Association of Educational Support Personnel, Head Start, the University of Louisville, and Image Enhancement Training for the physical plant employees at the University of Michigan. She participated in training for the Federally Employed Women (FEW) in both Kansas City, Kansas, and Cocoa Beach, Florida.

She is in partnership with the Girl Scouts were she teaches life skill lessons to middle school girls. One of her students once thanked her after the lesson because she stated that she didn't know the difference between a salad fork and a pitch fork, and her etiquette lesson enlightened her to the finer aspects of life. In conjunction with the Urban League and the University of Louisville, she produced a video and interviewed 21 entrepreneurs from 19 countries in Africa.

Norma started in the speaking field as a fashion commentator. She loved the craft of speaking so much in the beginning, that she literally would contract to speak for red roses and usually three chicken dinners, one for herself, her daughter and her mom.

To bring Norma Bryant Howard to your next event, contact:
Norma Bryant Howard
nhoward926@insightbb.com

Speeding Down the Highway to Success

Before I begin an extended car trip, I always visit the local AAA
Automobile Club and request a "Trip-Tik," which is a series of maps
bound together in a spiral booklet that marks the entire trip with a
colored highlighter from point of departure to point of destination.
The maps also indicate areas to purchase gas, food and lodging.
The agent places big red X's on parts of the map to show areas that
cause traffic delays and trouble. Some markings alert me to road
construction on your projected route. The agent advises that I should
be observant and watch out for any unexpected occurrences.

Imagine my utter confusion and frustration if I begin my trip without
these maps. I would head down the highway, miss the detour sign and
end up sitting beside the road construction crew!

Many people find themselves going through life without their own
personal "trip-tik". Your ticket for life simply must be goal setting.
Goals allow you to by-pass the big red X's of life, permit you to stay

focused and allow you to arrive at your destination in a timely fashion. Your life will move quicker down the highway to success and you will experience many of the joys life has to offer.

Some people carry desired goals in their heads. They quickly tell you it is not necessary to write goals down because it will be no problem focusing on a particular goal when the need arrives. With all the disorder most of us have in our heads, the last thing we need is to have something as important as our goals floating around with so many other important things. When we do not write down our goals it makes the road map of life fuzzy and vague, all of which leads to confusion, anger and unfulfilled dreams. Goal setting allows us to sort through the many choices we are presented with in life. Setting goals allows you to see the bigger picture you have set for your life.

Write your goals down. I repeat, write your goals down. It doesn't matter what kind of paper you write on, just write them down. Post them on the mirror, the dashboard, on the wall, anywhere you can see them on a daily basis. Most successful people will tell you they reviewed their goals regularly when they started down their personal road to success.

When I was a child my father's favorite expression was, "Think big!" He told all five children to set our minds on something, then dream big size dreams regarding it. Dad was a preacher, and if he was going to bring his congregation out of the country into the city, he had to dream his way out. He never used the word motivation but he lived his life, as a motivated person. As I look back on his life I now know he wanted us to be inspired by life, set our goals and allow us to dream "super size" dreams. And yes, the congregation did get to the city.

Instead of focusing on being a sales clerk at a local department store or working the front desk at the local hotel, set your course on one day owning a department store or a magnificent hotel.

You must believe you have the potential to reach desired goals. Turn a deaf ear to others who try to discourage you from reaching your dream. Believe with faith and persistence that you can make your goals a reality. Starting today you can overhaul your life and put yourself on the right road to success by following the five "road signs of life," that will help you reach your goals. So if you are ready, ladies and gentlemen it's time to start your engines!

STOP DEFEATING SELF-TALK

You simply must stop doing it! This is a huge road hazard that keeps you from reaching your goals. It is a form of negative conversations we have with ourselves, like a small tape recorder playing in our brains on a consistent basis. We say things like, "I know I will fail this test." "For generations, in my family, no one ever understood how to do mixed fractions." I have heard students say they hate themselves because they are fat, have bad hair, ugly skin or big noses. One student claimed she knew she was born for bad luck.

We can combat negative self-talk by doing something positive. Listen to motivational tapes, play positive music, read inspirational books and associate with positive people to re-program our negative self-talk. It has been stated that many people should not get up in the morning and listen to all the doom and gloom on morning news shows. This negative information usually sets the tone for the day. Have you ever awakened early in the morning and felt great? You heard birds outside your window and hints of spring or fall was in the air. As you savor the sweetness of the morning you turn on the national or local news and immediately hear a lot of depressing information. My son, when he was a pre-teen, said to me he did not like listening to the news at family dinnertime. We turned off the television and engaged in family conversation.

Start focusing on the positive and rid yourself of negative self-talk and negative stimulation. Whenever a negative thought jumps in your head, mentally say the word "cancel." It is a small technique but it does work.

STOP PROCRASTINATING!

You find yourself trying to park your dreams on the road side of life when you discover you are a victim of procrastination. I discovered that putting things off was the root of my very existence and was a huge road hazard for me. The word procrastination comes from the Latin verb procrastinare, meaning to put off until tomorrow. Now, if there was anything that I could do well as a youngster, it was put things off until tomorrow. Procrastination has its roots imbedded in a negative emotion and creates a lot of anxiety, guilt, and dread within its victims. When I was in college, I bought a book by an author who was describing the pitfalls of letting procrastination take over your life. Since I was the queen of procrastination, I allowed the book to sit on top of my bookcase for over a month because I was too "busy" procrastinating to read anything that had to do with the business of procrastination.

If you have not started your business selling "Grandma's pound cake" from her generation old recipe because you have been putting it off, you are losing out on a great gift that could be shared with the world. Do you spend time on the phone talking when you should be organizing your closet or office? I have found that being organized has helped me become more focused and is a way to keep procrastination at bay. Making a "to do" list and following it is also another useful tool. It provides an organized way of becoming aware of your tasks for the day, week or month. I use a simple method of using a sheet of 8 ½ x11 paper and fold it into thirds. I end up with a total of sixteen boxes (eight on the front and eight on the back). I have enough spaces for two weeks of task. Believe it or not it is a very useful system. Assigning a date to a task will enable you to commit to it. Using a day, week or monthly planner is also a very useful tool. Check off each item after you have completed it.

LOOKING FOR ASSISTANCE

Many people find it essential to have a life coach or mentor to encourage them along the hard knocks of life. Use a referral from an associate, an instructor or friend when looking for a mentor or go to the phone directory or "on-line" to find a coach in your area. You will find they are extremely useful for keeping you on track. I wanted to lose weight and found a diet center with a one-on-one counselor who encouraged and pushed me into keeping my goal of losing 25 pounds.

We all need someone who motivates us. Encouragers such as this make us feel more accountable for our actions.

DO NOT BLAME OTHERS

How ridiculous would it be if a motorist got out of his car and said to a police officer, "Officer, I would not have run into the back of that car if the house I glanced at had not had such a lovely front door? Sir, it is not my fault; it is the homeowner's fault because his door should not be so lovely!" Many people place blame on other people or other situations.

Some people feel the reason they have not accomplished anything significant in life is because other people either got in their way or were not encouraging enough. I know a lady who completed all of her requirements to become a high school principal. However, she never took that giant leap to interview with school personnel to complete the hiring process. Her excuse was that if her husband had been more supportive she would have become a principal. She felt it was easy to give up because it certainly was not her fault; it was her husband's. If you are guilty of doing this, you are shifting responsibility for your behavior to someone or something else.

Is there anything in your life that leads you to blame other people or situations and not take personal responsibility for what has happened in your life? Maybe it was a divorce, a lack of education, unloving parents, poverty, drugs, living with an extended family member (or no family member at all), not having enough money, any array of issues that many people confront in life. None of these is a sufficient reason to blame other people or situations for your failure to perform, achieve, and succeed.

Forgive yourself for feeling this way and decide you must move on with your life. Read inspirational books about people who accomplished outstanding things in life. People such as self-made millionaire, Madame C.J. Walker, Dr. Phil McGraw, expert in the field of human functioning and Les Brown, the motivator, are all people who rose from obscurity to heights of success and did not live their lives blaming others.

INTERRUPTIONS OR DISTRACTIONS

Interruptions or distractions have a way of making us travel a much more difficult road in life. It really is a form of procrastination because we are waiting for something to happen so we can postpone the task at hand. Many college students find themselves getting caught in this trap. They sit at their computers committed to doing their research. Suddenly the door opens and someone announces that the party is going on at the Forty-Forty Club. They drop everything and go to the party. This is the type of person who succumbs to interruptions and welcomes distractions. Deep down in their hearts they are wishing for a reason not to do the assignment. Many people will use the telephone as an excuse for not starting a project or visit their co-worker in the next cubicle to listen to the latest office gossip.

You must mentally think of the reasons why you should complete your task. There will always be time for fun. If possible write the reasons down on index cards and review them before you attempt doing the job. I had to move my upstairs office into the basement because I was easily distracted. My desk sat in front of the window. I found myself staring aimlessly out the window whenever I saw school children walking to school, making comments such as, "They are walking too slowly to school, surely they will be late", or "My goodness, I wonder who died because that certainly is a long funeral procession," or My God, look at the formation of those birds!" Needless to say when I moved my desk to the basement, with no windows in the room, my entire life changed for the best. It quickly changed my habit of being distracted.

Do something everyday to reach your destination in life. If you live on the east coast and want to drive to the west coast, you would not proceed from your hometown at dawn and expect to reach California by sun down. You would have to plan on getting there by reaching certain key cities within a certain amount of hours or days. If I wanted to climb to the top of the Empire State Building, I know I can not reach the top in a single leap, I realize I have to climb it step-by-step. So, it is with our dreams and aspirations. Accomplish your goals step-by-step. You can make it. Your trip down this mighty highway of life will have you arriving to your destination in record time and you will do it with your personal AAA Trip-Tik:

A= *ATTITUDE*

A= *ANALYZE*

A= *ACHIEVE*

Happy traveling! ⬆

Matthew C. Horne

240 605-1106

hornespeaks@yahoo.com

Matthew C. Horne is the last born child of Bernard and Valerie Horne, and is a native of Fort Washington, Md. He is a graduate of Coastal Carolina University where he attained a Bachelor of Arts Degree in English.

Matthew attended college on a full-athletic scholarship. He played four years of basketball at the Division I level. It is there where Matthew discovered his passion for motivational speaking.

Matthew has been privileged to speak in various arenas ranging from church organizations, businesses, to The U.S. Capitol. No matter the venue, the responses to his speeches are overwhelmingly similar. Here's what one of his latest clients has to say…
"You are well beyond your years in inferential reasoning; the ways in which you are able to recognize the pattern of success is unequivocal evidence of your maturity. Your motivational words encourage action and promote growth to any and all."
—India S. Thomas, President, Interior Consulting Group, Inc.

Matthew's speeches are often described as thought provoking and dynamic! This young motivational phenom is undoubtedly, as Les Brown would say, "not making a living, rather living his making."

Matthew has a commission to show the world how to live a life of OPTIMUM SUCCESS, as opposed to normal success. He implements his experiences on the basketball court to show people how to become not who they envision themselves being, or want to be, rather becoming everything they are pre-destined to be so they can live life at its' optimum. His message introduces people to their inner-genius, and removes barriers that separate people from their dreams.

Matthew's message caters to any age group or social background.

Matthew can be reached by calling 240-605-1106 or via e-mail at hornespeaks@yahoo.com

The Universe Is Inviting You In

"Dreams or desires don't just appear in your heart, they have purpose behind them and are designed by The Creator to be pursued for an outcome only He knows of."
—**Matthew Horne**

In this chapter, my objective is to enable you to gain an awareness of the world we exist in and the universe we're all designed to reside in. The Bible, what I call the greatest success manual ever assembled, states that "we are in the world, but not of the world." If we are in this world, but not of this world, then there must be a place that we're all supposed to reside in.

As I was riding up Massachusetts Avenue in Washington, DC, I noticed the different embassies. Each one of them had architecture that resembled the land which they represent. In essence, these ambassadors are in DC, but they're not of DC. They reside there, but are only subject to the laws of the land from which they were sent to represent...hence the term "diplomatic immunity."

Your dream, too, has diplomatic immunity in a sense. It's subject to the laws of your Creator who saw fit for you to exist in this earthly realm. The governing laws of this world may say that you aren't qualified, or you just don't meet the prerequisites required to achieve your dream. Your Creator says otherwise! Arriving 1 out of 400 million sperm is evidence that you're chosen and equipped. So many people don't pursue their dreams because they simply feel inadequate in some way, and have a deeply imbedded fear that their dreams will never be actualized. Yes, your dream may seem way out there, but at the same time it has instructions to thrive no matter what obstacles you face, internal or external.

If a blade of grass can permeate an insurmountable obstacle such as concrete, then your dream has the same capabilities. That seed of grass adheres to the instructions of its Creator and doesn't stop growing no matter the obstacle. Follow your dream and you will see that it too is subject to the same set of rules as the blade of grass. It will break through any illusionary barriers that may present themselves.

When you follow that dream, you'll see that providential forces have been enacted on your behalf as the events necessary to get you from where you are to your designed end are set in motion. Coincidence will become common place as your dream unfolds right in front of you. Being in the right place at the right time is a telling sign that you've entered the universe and stepped out of the world around you. Your dream is a first-class ticket out of the land of conformity with a destination to your best life possible.

Recognizing the dream in your heart and submitting to it is the first and most pivotal step to entering the universe and experiencing a life filled with amenities you only dreamed of! Just think for a second…of all the different routes you could have taken in life; all of the different things you could become in this grand universe, why is your heart pulling you in a specific direction? These are the types of questions great people ask themselves on a continual basis. I say "continual" because your heart is always pulling you in a direction that supercedes your current standing.

These are the questions that will pull you off your nine to five and walk you into your place within the universe. That dream in your heart is there for a reason. The desires you have, that don't go away in spite of circumstances that should have drowned them out by now, are still there because they are actually an extension of The Creator who saw fit for you to exist in this world. Your dream is your best output possible that you can give in this world. It is the best because your Creator is the only infallible existence there is. If He put an extension of Himself in you, then it is a can't-fail plan that will carry out something He has intended for you to do before you arrived here in this earthly realm. I hope that you can now begin to see that your dream isn't just another part of you, but the result of strategic placement by your Creator.

Separate Your Dream from You

Your dream is, like I mentioned above, an extension of God that resides in you. Once you really grasp that fact, then hesitancy will no longer exist. You will know that if your dream is something that is an extension of God, and not something your fallible self has manufactured, then the doubt will subside and contemplation on the perfect nature of this dream will resonate. If you put your faith in man or yourself, you'll be disappointed in some capacity every time; but if you put your faith in God, He'll do anything but fail.

Taking steps in the direction of your dream is putting absolute faith in your Creator. The way God designed it, everyone has some sort of dream or desire they want to fulfill in life. If you don't you're just not looking hard enough within! With the placement of this dream comes doubt and uncertainty concerning whether you can achieve it or not. This uncertainty is also the result of strategic placement. If you could just actualize your dream without internal and external opposition, there would be no need for you to have faith.

It is boldly stated in your Creator's **success manual** that "but without faith it is impossible to please him." With that being said, it's part of The Creator's plan that you will have to continually overcome doubt and opposition in the pursuit of your dream. Activating your dream is the initial act of faith that puts you in the ball game and sets you on your course to actualizing your dream! From start to finish, there is nothing you can do to qualify yourself to deserve having your dreams come to pass. The qualifier is simply having the faith to face the obstacles you'll encounter and believing that your Creator will see you through all of the rough spots, in spite of what your natural situation or circumstance indicates. For without faith it is impossible for your Creator to advance you to your next step in your dream pursuit.

The Truth of Your Dream

> "The dream that's in your heart may not necessarily be your IT in life, it may just be meant to put you in the vicinity of your TRUE IT!"
>
> —**Matthew Horne**

According to Robert Kiyosaki (Author of the "Rich Dad Poor Dad" series), "5 percent of the world's cash flow is generated by 95 percent of the world's working class population. Ninety-five percent of the world's cash flow is generated by business owners who only comprise 5 percent of the population." All cash flow is a derivative of someone's dream. Your lifetime earnings are contingent upon whether you'll support someone else's dream, or step into that 5th percentile who generate 95 percent of the world's income that just dared to believe in their dream!

When you make a conscious decision to follow your dream, you have done what the majority of society won't do! You're not on your way to success or failure, rather truth. As human beings, we will always have a desire to surpass our current condition resulting from our ever-evolving nature. There will be unrest within you, regardless of how much success or wealth you have attained, if you aren't exerting yourself in a way that facilitates you achieving more in life.

On life's journey you will find that some things that you envisioned yourself becoming represented the truth of who you are as you actualized what was once a dream. Dreams that facilitate success in the arena which they place you are truth. Some of the conceptions you have for yourself at the beginning of dream pursuit do not always materialize themselves. This isn't a bad thing! Any desire that's in your heart that you pursue until the end will actualize itself, or put you in the vicinity of some intricate part of yourself that The Creator knew you had all along, which is absolutely pivotal to fulfilling your destiny.

I entered college as an athletic 6'5" lights out shooter. I had a dream of becoming an NBA player. Given my physical attributes this wasn't unrealistic. This dream pursuit placed me at a university where I then found myself in a speech class with people marveling at a speech that I just threw together. Five of these people then pulled me to the side and told me, with the most genuine looks of sincerity I've ever seen, that I should be a motivational speaker. This now places me writing an empowering message to you!

I had a dream of becoming an NBA player, which I can say retrospectively thinking was there for a reason. It didn't actualize itself, but it revealed a truth about me that was undeniably the key to me fulfilling my destiny. Don't be disappointed when things didn't go the way you envisioned them going at the onset of your dream pursuit. I'll guarantee you that if you see your dreams through until the end you will have emerged into the very thing The Creator knew you were before the foundation of this world. Truth is the only permeating element at the end of dream pursuit, not success or failure. That's why I say with confidence that you must pursue the dream that is in your heart! Dreams are the path way to discovering your true existence and becoming everything The Creator has intended for you to be. When you're everything your Creator already knows you are, it is then and only then, that you live life at its optimum. I say this because you are incapable of manufacturing a plan for your life that could rival the one The Creator has laid out for you.

The *success manual* clearly states that "there is a way that seemeth right to a man, but the end thereof is death." This isn't a physical death so to speak, but a death that will qualify you as a walking corpse. When you step outside of your pre-destined genetic makeup and attempt to find success there, it is never whole. The Creator's path is laid out in such a way that you will not only have the financial amenities that qualify you as a "success," but you will also have the inner-peace that can only be attributed to occupying your designed space within the universe.

I know everyone has been exposed to someone who seemingly has it all: the house; the cars; the luxuries that our society defines as success, but you can look at their everyday actions and demeanor and tell something is missing. Yes, something is missing, the internal peace and soundness of mind that comes along with submitting to THE

PLAN for your life and not manufacturing "a plan" and calling it success when it becomes reality. I heard a wise man say something that kept me in the ball game many of times when I wanted to fold in my hand and attain my dreams my way. He said "The most evil thing you could do is knowingly walk away from the will of God on your life."He then said "Evil manifests itself in the end." People think they can create a plan that's better than the one The Creator has laid out for them, but if and when they actually attain it, they see that there is something missing, which is then relayed to us with a look of disparity in the midst of what society defines as " lavish lifestyle."

The universe is always giving you signs that point you in the direction of your space within it. It's no coincidence when people are constantly bringing your effortless gifts to your attention. Often times these effortless gifts have a direct correlation to the desires of your heart. An inclined ear to the whispers of the universe is a prelude to discovering your true existence. The sole objective for our creation is that we occupy our space within this universe we exist in. Following that dream in your heart may appear to you, and others around you, as taking steps backwards, but in all actuality you are taking gargantuan leaps in the direction of your space within the universe…leaps in the direction of your best life possible!

If there's still any question about anything I've said within this chapter, just look at the Oscars and listen to the speech pattern of all the award recipients when they step on stage… (Tears streaming down their face) It all started with a dream… I was just a…! If you follow your dream and uncompromisingly see it through, your speech will too sound something like this: It all started with a dream… I was just a…! ⬆

Joey Smith

joey@higherhill.com

www.joey-smith.com

Joey Smith has well over a decade of fast-paced and laser-focused experience in technology management in various industries. These include training, development, technology consulting, telecommunications, media communications, manufacturing, distribution, wholesale and retail. While achieving personal effectiveness and business success, he has gained extensive experience in developing leaders, excellence programs, quality training and customer service.

Smith, a man who understands business and the bottom line, has solid technology skills demonstrated by his Enterprise Architecture certification and various Microsoft certifications. He has implemented extensive Microsoft technologies and won the 1999 Microsoft Project of the Year in the Knowledge Management category as well as the Microsoft Pinnacle award for Best Innovative ERM Solution in 2003. He also has experience in assessing a company's technology strategy and capacity, formulating a vision and operating plan that supports senior management's business objectives, and implementing the projects that bring true value to the business owners. Additionally, his business growth related skills have played a critical role in achieving Fortune Top 50 Fastest Growing Company status.

Smith has utilized master principles of project management while leading the technology strategy, support, research, development and software deployment for major corporations such as Cox Communications and Coca Cola Enterprises. He has assisted companies in many high return technology initiatives like ecommerce, knowledge management, intranet, extranet, disaster recovery, security, CRM and ERM. Smith's success has led to the "first time in history" two-time finalist status for the Georgia CIO of the Year in 2003 and 2004.

Finally, Smith has a passion for leadership and teamwork development. His leadership success led to winning the John Maxwell (author of the 21 Irrefutable

Laws of Leadership) Leadership Award in 2001. His gift of communication allows him to share deep insights and critical information in bite-size chunks that are easily digested and absorbed by the technically and non-technically inclined. This ability led to the creation of the only international success training system for IT Managers called the IT Manager Success University. Smith's style, commitment and passion are what make him a highly sought after speaker, facilitator, trainer, coach and author to both the IT and Non-IT communities.

Email joey@higherhill.com for speaking engagements, corporate retreats, strategic consulting, article requests or collaboration. For more information, go to http://www.joey-smith.com/

Join the Top 1% of the World through a Commitment to Excellence

"We are what we repeatedly do. Excellence, then, is not an act but a habit."
—**Aristotle**

When I was a kid, my sister made a habit of calling me stupid. And since we are what we repeatedly do—or hear—I made a habit of believing I was stupid. After all, I had no reason to dispute her affectionate nickname for me. She was two years older than me; made straight A's in school and planned to be a teacher. I made mediocre grades at best because of my belief and so decided to focus on music, not academics.

My average grades and expertise in music managed to get me into the same college as my sister. One day, she challenged me to an IQ test being sponsored by the Mensa Club. I'm not sure why I agreed to a test which would measure my brain power against hers, but I did. The results shocked us both.

My score was 23 points higher than my sister's. Immediately I felt intelligent and began to apply myself in a different way than ever before. Not only did I surpass my sister's scores in her toughest subjects, I learned to achieve perfect and higher than perfect scores and amazed my teachers in the process. I dropped out of music and took up philosophy and psychology and eventually business.

I felt as though I had been freed from prison. But why? I was the same person with the same mind the day after the test as I was the day before the test. I looked the same. I acted the same. I hung out with the same people. Only my grades were drastically improved. I would strive for 100, then do the bonus questions. My grades shot up to 106 and 112 averages. It became fun, and my peers dubbed me a geek. That title made me proud.

For the first time in my life, I was the teacher's favorite and maintained a 100+ average. Not in just one or two subjects, but in everything I took: math, accounting, computers, philosophy, psychology, history and economics. How could that be? I was supposed to be a poorly paid starving artist, not a geek like my sister. Then I started asking myself a different question. I started asking myself how I could apply this quest for excellence to every aspect of my life, including music.

The first thing I realized is that excellence requires commitment. It is this commitment which separates successful people from average people. Average people may want and expect excellence, but they don't understand it enough to become committed to achieving it.

We all understand commitment in terms of loyalty to friendships, marriage and work. Commitment, however, is really the state of being bound emotionally or intellectually to someone, some thing or some ideal (i.e. Person, Passion or Purpose). It is the principle and ideal of excellence that we have to be emotionally and intellectually bound to. In essence, it is the act of creating a contract or a binding obligation with "excellence." Mark McCormack, founder and CEO of International Management Group (IMG), the sports management conglomerate that represents Tiger Woods, Wayne Gretzky, Arnold Palmer and Andre Agassi, once said, "Commit yourself to excellence from day one…it's better to do nothing at all than to do something badly." The keyword here is commitment.

After I understood the commitment required, I sought an understanding of the subject. Excellence is brilliance. Excellence is distinction. Excellence is superiority. Excellence is perfection. Excellence is greatness. Excellence goes beyond the status quo and against the norm. Warren G. Bennis once said, "Excellence is a better teacher than mediocrity. The lessons of the ordinary are everywhere. Truly profound and original insights are to be found only in studying the exemplary."

As it relates to business, the company's level of excellence determines sales. In order to achieve legendary status, businesses have to be superb at what they do. People don't say, "Hey, let's go get an okay steak," or "Let's go to a second-rate party." You do not and will not hear such things because people expect excellence from the businesses they buy from.

Excellence is also ongoing. It is not a position, place or achievement. No one arrives at excellence for excellence is not a destination. Tom Peters, a renowned business philosopher, said, "Excellent firms don't believe in excellence—only in constant improvement and constant change." He also went on to say, "If it isn't broke, you just haven't looked hard enough. Fix it anyway." Excellence, therefore, is a state of mind. To be excellent, you have to be willing and determined to raise your standards and be better today than you were yesterday.

So how do you accomplish excellence? Simple. Change your thought process.

From a very young age, we are conditioned by our parents, siblings, teachers, peers and media to accept mediocrity. It starts with our grading system, a system which promotes average work. I lived shackled in that system for years, a C student who believed he had no potential, no hope, no chance for success. I was average, and I thought that's who I always had to be. Until I saw those test scores. Something inside me clicked at that moment, and I recognized I could be excellent.

My recognition of the fact that I could be excellent is what changed my life. I recognized it because my eyes and ears were WIDE open, and I caught what it meant to achieve excellence. The same holds true for you. Excellence can only be achieved when you are present and focused. When I say present, I mean being actively engaged in the moment. Have you ever played a sport, won, but were not sure why? What about winning and knowing it was in the bag? What was the difference? Your eyes were "WIDE" open. You were confident because you were focused and present. You knew winning was a certainty and were relentless in its pursuit.

Even while you are reading this chapter, your mind is processing a million things. You are thinking about that meeting you have this morning, that place you are going for lunch, that phone call you need to make, that bill you have to pay. Am I right? Admit it. How many of you have thought about these things and more while reading this chapter?

Most workers are only 20% productive throughout the entire day. This is true because we are continually distracted by our environment, our beliefs, our passions, our desires, our pains, etc. Yoga and other forms of martial arts were formed to capture present focus and to free the mind of distraction. When the mind is free from distraction, excellence becomes possible.

Pain is also used sometimes to pull the mind back to the present. For instance, NLP (Neuro-Linguistic-Programing), if implemented in the correct way, is used to gain present focus. For instance, a popular NLP technique to use after an incorrect behavior pattern is observed is to snap a rubber band on the wrist to get the mind back to the present in order to be corrected. This is a method of training your mind to get rid of unwanted habits. As it pertains to Yoga, certain poses were created to generate pain or to position your body off center to keep the mind focused on the present. This is called heightened awareness or body-form meditation. The pain method works. Try it. The next time you start to fall asleep but want to stay awake, slap yourself in the face or pinch your arm. You will be sure to regain your focus instantly.

Thomas J. Watson said, "If you want to achieve excellence, you can get there today. As of this second, quit doing less-than-excellent work." It is that simple. It is almost like believing in something that you can't see, touch or feel. It is not that you have to see it to believe it. You have to believe in order to make it happen. You have to be targeted and focused.

What is the difference maker for you? Has it clicked for you yet? Do you know that excellence is in you by design? You already have it. Just like me. Remember, I wasn't biologically different before and after the IQ test, but knowing who I was opened the lock to unlimited potential. The real kicker is that it didn't matter what the IQ test said anyway. If you score low, I would challenge that the actual test results could be a part of your programming and subconscious belief system. For some reason that day I was open to the possibility. Remember, you have that same potential because you are human and excellence is in your DNA. Buckminster Fuller, Einstein's apprentice once said "I am convinced all of humanity is born with more gifts than we know. Most are born geniuses and just get de-geniused rapidly.

I believe that everyone is capable of 110% on every subject. Sure, some things are easier than others, but the difference maker is your ability to be present and focused with your "eyes wide open." In order to be present, your attitude has to change. You have to want it and believe it. That is why attitude determines altitude and ultimately determines excellence.

What is your attitude towards excellence? Are you the best in your current capacity? If not, you could be. It is all about a commitment, an understanding and a belief. Excellence is with you now. You have it. You were born with it. It is not something you learn, although you see it and experience it everyday. It is so innate you recognize it when you see it. You also expect it from others. So just do it and you will never be the same. Insist on excellence with all of your suppliers, vendors, managers, employees, etc. It is inherently in each and every one of them. It is limiting beliefs that are keeping it from them and from you.

What do you believe about yourself? Are you capable of being the best in your field? Don't settle for average in yourself. Analyze and examine all of your limiting beliefs, because they are holding you back from acquiring excellence. Once you break down these barriers, exemplify excellence and practice it daily through concentrated effort. This truly will set you apart and elevate you to the top 1% of your peers.

Excellence is a habit. And you can learn how to acquire this habit. So will you? Will you commit to a habit of excellence today and join the top?

If this chapter has changed your view or your life in anyway, please drop me a quick email at joey@higherhill.com. I would love to hear from you! ⬆

Kevin Bracy

877 210 2676

kevin@kevinbracy.com

www.kevinbracy.com

Kevin has delivered messages for organizations such as 24 Hour Fitness, Hewlett Packard, SBC, Cal Trans, and Colonial Life Insurance. He has also enjoyed speaking to over 300,000 high school and college students across the country and has been privileged to speak at the T.D. Jakes Megafest Conference two years in a row. Kevin takes the opportunity to touch lives very seriously, he speaks on the subjects of motivation, leadership, diversity, overcoming obstacles, goal setting and change.

Kevin learned the importance of nurturing dreams at an early age after overcoming a difficult childhood. Despite his early life challenges, Kevin went on to earn a baseball scholarship to the University of Utah, acquired three college degrees, played two years of professional baseball in Canada and is now a successful speaker and entrepreneur.

Currently, Kevin runs a coaching program for professional speakers that spans across the United States as well as the United Kingdom and Jamaica. Within one year he helped over sixty speakers become authors while writing two books of his own. Kevin has read and researched over 1,000 books on leadership, communication, sales and peak performance and has built a successful networking team, leading hundreds of independent business owners through the daily challenges of business ownership.

Massive Motivation...Massive Change

Peter Drucker calls this time we live in the era of the three C's...
accelerated Change, overwhelming Complexity and tremendous
Competition. Things are changing at the speed of light, maybe faster
than ever before. People move and change jobs more now than in
times past. Schools change their curriculum. Sports teams leave one
city and go to another. Technology is breaking new territory every
day. You buy a new cell phone today and a new version comes out
tomorrow. New cameras, recorders, computer software, child safety
devices, kitchen tools and car designs appear nearly every day. Did you
know it took 13 years from the time television was introduced until
there were fifty million viewers? It took 26 years for radio to get fifty
million listeners. It only took five years for the internet to get fifty
million people online. There's some CHANGE for sure and rapid
CHANGE at that.

As of right now, there are hundreds of thousands more emails being
sent daily than letters going through the post office. CHANGE.

When you fly these days you can get your boarding pass from a computer rather than a live person. CHANGE.

We recently checked into a hotel through a computer. We typed in our information and the machine spit out the key. CHANGE.

The ancient Greek philosopher Aristotle talked about change being the most frightening thing in the world. He was right, that's true. But it's also true that change is an inevitable part of each of our lives. Change is something you can count on happening, coming at us, being with us throughout our lives. No matter what we do, or where we go, change is sure to be part of our journey.

To embrace change, we must first understand it. The dictionary defines "change" in a few ways—"to make or become different, to replace with another; the act, process or result of changing." The dictionary helps us to define the word, but it does not help us to deal with the changes in our lives.

Change is frightening, as Aristotle pointed out so long ago. It's about having to unplug from the old and plug into the new—that can be scary. When we're faced with change, we are often faced with unknowns. It is normal to fear the unknown. It isn't change we fear as much as the transition that occurs from where we are and what we know to where we might be headed and what might be involved. We don't know what's coming; don't know if we can handle it, if we are smart enough, if it will work out, or if the change really will be, as people often say, "for the best". Not knowing may account for that feeling of fear, but we can't let the fear win.

Motivation appears when you understand change…Accept it, Adapt to it, Embrace it and Grown from it!

Understanding change means understanding the stages of transition. It is necessary to accept the fact that life is changing; we can't control it so we need to understand it. Many of our kids don't know what a vinyl record is, yet 20 years ago that was how we listened to music. Can you imagine a car or a house without air conditioning? That too was a change that occurred. Once we realize that change is a constant in life, and that it is happening all of the time, then we can then learn to accept it, adapt to it, embrace it and watch the personal growth that comes from it.

We really don't have much choice about accepting change. It's life!

We are creatures who adapt. Once we accept change, we adapt to it. When the weather becomes cold we put on a jacket. Years ago, when Bill Gates predicted there would be computer on every desktop in America, people laughed. Today, futurists are saying, not only will every business have computers, but relatively soon there will be more computers in the homes of Americans than televisions.

Accepting change allows us then to embrace it. And this is where the motivation comes in. Embracing change gives us the freedom to experience the journey. Once we embrace the change, we are able to gain the motivation to go through the phases and make our way to the growth stage. Growth comes from the journey, from the fear, the pain and from the realization that change is going to happen no matter what. When we've accepted the idea of change we can begin to adapt to it, embrace it and focus on growing through the change rather than just going through it.

I have experienced many big changes in my life, as most people have. I am who I am today because of the events in my life, the choices I have made and the changes I've absorbed.

One big life changing event came in the form of a baseball scholarship to the University of Utah. I vividly remember the moment I opened the letter, I had been offered a baseball scholarship, and a dream come true! I remember being filled with excitement which was quickly replaced by fear...I had no family or friends in Utah, I was entering into the unknown.

The change took place in the 9 hour car ride from California to Utah. I went from frightened to ready to tackle the challenges...from *can I do this* to *of course I can*. The change was complete; I had arrived in Utah, now I had to deal with the transition. All of the sudden I was responsible for myself! I had made the decision to go to the University of Utah, away from my friends and family, now I had to adapt, and I had to do it quickly, I had no other choice! If I wanted clean clothes I had to wash them. If I was hungry, I had to first go to the grocery store and then cook (microwave) my food.

I understood what I had to do; soon I began to embrace the change. I became more motivated through this experience. The fear I had experienced was replaced with a sense of adventure; I was beginning to enjoy the journey. I finally began to see the growth I was making because of the change. It became natural for me to pay my bills, clean my apartment and take care of myself. I had met the challenge, embraced it, and made it my own. And it, in return, helped me to grow. It gave me new skills, new ways to validate myself, new opportunities to stretch and accomplish—ways I would never have experienced if I had resisted the change, given in to the fear.

To Get From Change To Success

There are five steps to familiarize yourself with as you are experiencing change. They will help you remember the purpose for change and put your journey in perspective. As you experience the emotions of your journey remember these steps and use them as tools to guide you along your way.

1. **It's Do-able**
    Developing ourselves personally, growing is the result of change. It is a fact that you would not be he person you are becoming today if you had not gone through the changes and challenges you have experienced in your life. Understand the stages of transition—the fear, followed by acceptance, adapting and embracing change—will give you the confidence to know that, when any type of change occurs, it's do-able. When faced with sudden change, most people's first thought is that they can't do whatever it is that the change involves. We tend to become overwhelmed and view the process as impossible; however, what we have discovered is that there is no such thing as impossible.

    Impossible is a big word thrown around by small men and women who find it easier to live with the life they have been given than to explore within themselves for a way to change it. Impossible is not a declaration, it is a dare. It is not a fact, it is an opinion. Impossible is not a winners reality, it is a winners mission to overcome. Impossible is nothing.

2. **It's a Must**

   Since change is inevitable and unavoidable; it's wise to BRACE yourself for a change, create a mental suit of armor so when change comes your way you have the protection to handle it. There are a few things you can do on a regular basis to BRACE yourself for change. Put "positives" in your life, read books, listen to CD's full of motivation, inspiration, and empowering information to talk you up. Talk to yourself daily; have affirmations you say to yourself to move yourself toward greatness—"stir yourself up". Monitor who you are spending time with; where they are going; and what their goals and dreams are. Put yourself in the best place for your own well being and development. Albert Einstein said, "The significant challenges we face in life cannot be solved at the same level of thinking we were at when we created them." We must raise our levels of thinking; take ourselves from the problems mentality to the possibilities mentality. We need to know we can and that we will change and grow from changing.

3. **It's a Challenge**

   Change can be uncomfortable. Leaving our comfort zone is a true test of our self-esteem and our self-image. In a recent study done on Harvard graduates, 70% said it was a lack of self-esteem that kept them from moving into their desired career paths. Lack of self-esteem can be an enormous stumbling block, but it doesn't have to be. The challenge is to find those barriers that keep us from growing through change and try to erase them if we can. At the very least, we can challenge ourselves to work around them if we can't erase them completely. It is not always easy, but if we view the experience as a challenge with a victory at the end, it will change the entire tone of the journey.

4. **It Is Your Responsibility**

   It is your responsibility to understand and recognize where you are in your life and in the phases of change. If you were to drive your car in the dark without your headlights, it would be extremely hard to tell where you are going. How would you know where to turn or when to put the brakes on? The same goes for the phases of change—if you go through them without knowing where you are or where you have been, it makes for a much bumpier ride. *Recognizing what phase you are in goes a long way to smoothing out the transition.* This is one of those things no one else can do for you; only you can take you to the level of understanding where you are.

5. It's Life Changing

There is not doubt—Change will affect your life. Sometimes change will be negative, other times positive. But most certainly change is a part of life and changes can and will have long lasting effects. Change is what happens to us throughout life. Change is how we learn and grow. Change is how we move from where we are today to where we will be tomorrow. It is a true statement that it is not what happens in your life that matters, but how you deal with it. Try looking at change as a journey, an adventure. That may simplify the process and take some of the fear away. Remind yourself, without change there is no growth. Change breeds new beginnings and new opportunities. Let's remember that along with the challenges come great rewards—personal, professional, experiential, and since we all have to go through the changes, and have to experience change, we really owe it to ourselves to enjoy the trip! ♠

"You will be on the journey longer than you'll be at the destination, is it is imperative to enjoy the journey!"
—**Unknown**